HUMOROUS POETRY
FOR
CHILDREN

HUMOROUS POETRY

FOR CHILDREN

EDITED BY

WILLIAM COLE

ILLUSTRATED BY

ERVINE METZL

COLLINS

Published by William Collins Publishers Inc.
2080 West 117th Street, Cleveland, Ohio 44111

ISBN #0-529-03480-8

LIBRARY OF CONGRESS CATALOG CARD NUMBER: 55-5283

Copyright Acknowledgments

The editor and The World Publishing Company herewith render thanks to the following authors, publishers and agents whose interest, cooperation and permission to
reprint have made possible the preparation of *Humorous Poetry for Children*. All possible care has been taken to trace the ownership of every selection included and to
make full acknowledgment for its use. If any errors have accidentally occurred they
will be corrected in subsequent editions, provided notification is sent to the publisher.

Appleton-Century-Crofts, Inc., for "A Seaside Romance" and "The Jokesmith's Vaca-
tion" from *Noah an' Jonah an' Cap'n John Smith*, by Don Marquis, copyright, 1921,
D. Appleton & Co.; for "A College Training" from *Cape Cod Ballads*, by Joseph C.
Lincoln, copyright, 1910, D. Appleton & Co.; for "A Bachelor of Maine," by Ellen
Douglas Deland, from the *St. Nicholas Book of Verse*, copyright, 1923, The Century
Company. Reprinted by permission of the publishers Appleton-Century-Crofts, Inc.

Edward Arnold, Ltd., for "Patience," "Presence of Mind," and "Quiet Fun" from
More Ruthless Rhymes, by Harry Graham, published by G. P. Putnam's Sons. Reprinted by permission of Edward Arnold, Ltd.

Brandt & Brandt, for "in Just spring" from *Poems 1923–1954*, by E. E. Cummings,
copyright, 1923, 1954, by E. E. Cummings, published by Harcourt, Brace and Company, Inc.

Curtis Brown, Ltd., for "Jonathan Bing" from *Jonathan Bing and Other Verses*, by
B. Curtis Brown, published by Oxford University Press, Inc., copyright, 1936, by
Beatrice Curtis Brown, reprinted by permission of the author.

Robert Clairmont, for "The Answers" from *Forever X*, by Robert Clairmont, copyright, 1951, Robert Clairmont, published by Contemporary Poetry.

D. E. Collins, for "A Dedication" from *Greybeards at Play*, by G. K. Chesterton,
published by Sheed and Ward, Inc., New York. Reprinted by permission of the
executive of Mr. Chesterton's estate and Sheed and Ward.

J. B. Lippincott Company, for "Stairs" from *Excuse It Please*, by Oliver Herford, copyright, 1929, by Oliver Herford, published by J. B. Lippincott Company.

Little, Brown & Company, for "Adventures of Isabel," "Arthur," "The Lama," and "The Rhinoceros" from *Many Long Years Ago*, by Ogden Nash, copyright, 1936, 1940, 1931, 1933, Ogden Nash; for "The Octopus" from *Good Intentions*, by Ogden Nash, copyright, 1942, Ogden Nash; for "The Purist" from *I'm a Stranger Here Myself*, by Ogden Nash, copyright, 1942, Ogden Nash.

Liveright Publishing Corporation, for "The Gnu" from *Poems in Praise of Practically Nothing*, by Samuel Hoffenstein, copyright, 1928, Samuel Hoffenstein, reprinted by permission of Liveright Publishers, New York.

Hughes Mearns, for "The Little Man Who Wasn't There" and "The Perfect Reactionary," by Hughes Mearns; for "Skip-scoop-anellie," by Tom Prideaux, and "Johnny," by Emma Rounds, from *Creative Youth: An Anthology of Lincoln School Verse*, by Hughes Mearns, published by Doubleday Page & Company. Reprinted by permission of the author.

New Directions, for "*From* Under Milk Wood" from *Under Milk Wood*, by Dylan Thomas, copyright, 1954, by New Directions, reprinted with the permission of the copyright owner.

Preston Newman, for "Some Questions To Be Asked of a Rajah, Perhaps by the Associated Press," by Preston Newman, which appears on page 101 of this volume, copyright, 1953, The New Yorker Magazine, Inc.

L. C. Page & Company, for "In Foreign Parts" from *The Piccolo*, by Laura E. Richards, copyright, L. C. Page & Company.

The Proprietors of Punch, for "Request Number," by G. N. Sprod, from *Punch*, issue of November 21, 1951, reprinted by permission of the Proprietors of Punch; for "The Uses of Ocean," by Sir Owen Seaman, from *Punch*, issue of July 29, 1914, reprinted by permission of the Proprietors of Punch.

The Proprietors of Punch and A. P. Watt & Son, for "Save the Tiger!" from *Laughing Ann*, by Sir A. P. Herbert, copyright, 1926, by Doubleday & Company, Inc. Reprinted by permission of the author, the Proprietors of Punch, and Ernest Benn, Ltd.

G. P. Putnam's Sons, for "Blum" from *Here, There and Everywhere*, by Dorothy Aldis, copyright, 1927, Dorothy Aldis; for "Our Silly Little Sister" from *All Together*, by Dorothy Aldis, copyright, 1952, Dorothy Aldis; for "Ozymandias Revisited" and "The Tales the Barbers Tell" from *Paramount Poems*, by Morris Bishop, copyright, 1929, Morris Bishop, published by Minton, Balch & Co.

Trustee u/w Laura E. Richards, for "Antonio," by Laura E. Richards, from Child Life Magazine, copyright, 1936, Child Life Magazine, reprinted by permission of the Trustee u/w Laura E. Richards.

E. V. Rieu, for "Hall and Knight or $z+b+x=y+b+z$" from *Cuckoo Calling*, by E. V. Rieu, published by Menthuen & Co., London, reprinted by permission of the author.

Charles Scribner's Sons, for "The Song of Mr. Toad" from *The Wind in the Willows*, by Kenneth Grahame, copyright, 1908, 1913, 1933, 1953, by Charles Scribner's Sons, reprinted by permission of the publishers.

Charles Scribner's Sons and Jonathan Cape, Ltd., for "The Shades of Night" and "Inhuman Henry or Cruelty to Fabulous Animals," by A. E. Housman, from *My*

For

PEGGY

CONTENTS

INTRODUCTION 15

Anonymous
To Be or Not To Be 21
The Common Cormorant 21
Rhyme for a Simpleton 21
The Groaning Board 21
After Oliver 22
Poor Old Lady 22
Get Up, Get Up 22
Mr. Finney's Turnip 22
Aunt Maud 23
As I Was Standing in the
    Street 23
Peas 23
Jaybird 23
Old Farmer Buck 23
O I C 24
The Prodigal Egg 24
Nirvana 24
The Microbes 24
As I Was Laying on the
    Green 24
Stately Verse 25
The Kilkenny Cats 25
I'm a Little Hindoo 25
A Centipede Was Happy
    Quite 25
Tails 26
Conversational 26
Brian O'Linn 26
Rumbo and Jumbo 27
Young Sammy Watkins 28
Sister Nell 28
Willie the Poisoner 28
Careless Willie 28

Limericks
An Epicure, Dining at
    Crewe 28

There Was an Old Man
    from Antigua 28
A Maiden Caught Stealing
    a Dahlia 28
There Was a Young Man
    So Benighted 28
There Was a Young Man
    of Herne Bay 28
A Silly Young Fellow
    Named Hyde 29
There Was an Old Man of
    Tarentum 29
There Was an Old Person
    of Tring 29
A Decrepit Old Gasman,
    Named Peter 29
A Flea and a Fly in a Flue 29
A Boy Who Played Tunes
    on a Comb 29
There Was an Old Man of
    Blackheath 29

Franklin P. Adams (1881-1960)
The Rich Man 29

Dorothy Aldis (1897-   )
Blum 30
Our Silly Little Sister 30

N. P. Babcock (19th Century)
The Stranger Cat 30

Hilaire Belloc (1870-1953)
The Yak 31
G 31
The Frog 32
The Hippopotamus 32
George 32

John Bennett (1865-1958)
A Tiger's Tale 33

[9]

Morris Bishop (1893-   )
  Song of the Pop-bottlers   33
  Ozymandias Revisited   34
  The Tales the Barbers Tell   34

Isaac H. Bromley (1833-1898)
  The Passenjare   35

B. Curtis Brown (20th Century)
  Jonathan Bing   35

Gelett Burgess (1866-1951)
  I Wish That My Room Had
    a Floor   36
  The Purple Cow   36
  Tricky   36

W. A. Butler (1825-1902)
  Tom Twist   36

C. S. Calverley (1831-1884)
  Love   38
  From Morning   38

Lewis Carroll (1832-1898)
  Father William   39
  He Thought He Saw   40
  The Walrus and the
    Carpenter   40
  Ways and Means   42
  From The Hunting of the
    Snark   43

Charles Edward Carryl (1841-
  1920)
  The Walloping Window-
    blind   48
  The Highlander's Song   48
  Robinson Crusoe's Story   49
  The Post Captain   49

Guy Wetmore Carryl (1873-
  1904)
  The Fearful Finale of the
    Irascible Mouse   51
  Little Red Riding Hood   52

The Sycophantic Fox and
    the Gullible Raven   53

G. K. Chesterton (1874-1936)
  A Dedication   54

Robert Clairmont (1902-   )
  The Answers   54

E. E. Cummings (1894-1962)
  in Just spring   55

Walter de la Mare (1873-1956)
  Bones   55

Ellen Douglas Deland (1860-
  1923)
  A Bachelor of Maine   55

T. S. Eliot (1888-1965)
  The Naming of Cats   56

Anthony Euwer (1877-   )
  My Face   57

Eugene Field (1850-1895)
  The Little Peach   57

Samuel Foote (1720-1777)
  The Great Panjandrum   57

Sam Walter Foss (1858-1911)
  The Prayer of Cyrus Brown   58

Mary E. Wilkins Freeman
  (1852-1930)
  The Ostrich Is a Silly Bird   58

Norman Gale (1862-1942)
  Bobby's First Poem   58
W. S. Gilbert (1836-1911)
  The Policeman's Lot   59
  The Yarn of the Nancy Bell   59
  From The Lord Chancel-
    lor's Song   61
  Captain Reece   62
  The Duke of Plaza-Toro   63
  Etiquette   64

[10]

General John 66
There Was a Young Man of
  St. Bees 67

Harry Graham (1874-1936)
Common Sense 67
Patience 67
Tragedy 67
Presence of Mind 68
Quiet Fun 68

Kenneth Grahame (1859-1932)
The Song of Mr. Toad 68

Arthur Guiterman (1871-1943)
The Legend of the First
  Cam-u-el 68
Qwerty-ù-i-op 69
Routine 70
In Praise of Llamas 70
Habits of the Hippopotamus 71

Bret Harte (1839-1902)
Plain Language from Truth-
  ful James 71

Sir A. P. Herbert (1890-   )
Save the Tiger! 72

Oliver Herford (1863-1935)
Stairs 73
The Crocodile 73
Japanesque 74
The Unfortunate Giraffe 74
The Artful Ant 74

Samuel Hoffenstein (1890-1947)
The Gnu 76

Oliver Wendell Holmes (1809-
1894)
The Height of the
  Ridiculous 76
From The September Gale 76

Thomas Hood (1799-1845)
From A Parental Ode to My

Son, Aged Three Years
  and Five Months 77
No! 78
Faithless Nancy Gray 78

A. E. Housman (1859-1936)
The Shades of Night 79
Inhuman Henry or Cruelty
  to Fabulous Animals 80

Wallace Irwin (1875-1959)
A Dash to the Pole 80
The Rhyme of the Chival-
  rous Shark 81
Sensitive Sydney 82
The Fate of the Cabbage
  Rose 83

Henry Johnstone (1844- ?)
The Fastidious Serpent 83

John Keats (1795-1821)
There Was a Naughty Boy 84

Ben King (1857-1894)
The Pessimist 84
If I Should Die Tonight 85
That Cat 85
The Cow Slips Away 85

Edward Lear (1812-1888)
The New Vestments 86
Incidents in the Life of My
  Uncle Arly 87
The Two Old Bachelors 87
From The Jumblies 88
The Pobble Who Has No
  Toes 89
There Was an Old Man
  with a Beard 90
There Was a Young Lady
  Whose Eyes 90
There Was an Old Person
  of Dundalk 90
There Was an Old Man of
  Ibreem 90

[11]

How Pleasant to Know Mr.
Lear 90

Henry S. Leigh (1837-1883)
The Twins 91

Newman Levy (1888-1966)
The Revolving Door 91

Joseph C. Lincoln (1870-1944)
A College Training 92

Frederick Locker-Lampson
(1821-1895)
A Terrible Infant 93

Don Marquis (1878-1937)
A Seaside Romance 93
The Jokesmith's Vacation 94
archy a low brow 95
From certain maxims of
archy 96
the hen and the oriole 96
the honey bee 96
From archy s autobiography 97

Hughes Mearns (1875-1965)
The Little Man Who
Wasn't There 97
The Perfect Reactionary 97

A. A. Milne (1882-1956)
Bad Sir Brian Botany 97

Cosmo Monkhouse (1840-1901)
The Barber of Kew 98
The Girl of New York 98

Ogden Nash (1902-   )
The Lama 98
Adventures of Isabel 98
The Purist 99
The Octopus 99
The Rhinoceros 100
Arthur 100

Joseph S. Newman (1891-1960)
Baby Kate 100
The Concert 100

Preston Newman 1913-1961)
Some Questions To Be
Asked of a Rajah, Per-
haps by the Associated
Press 101

Alfred Noyes (1880-1958)
Daddy Fell into the Pond 101

Walter Parke (19th Century)
His Mother-in-law 102
There Was a Young Prince
in Bombay 102
There Was an Old Stupid
Who Wrote 102

M. Pelham (19th Century)
The Comical Girl 102

William Pitt (? -1840)
The Sailor's Consolation 103

Anna M. Pratt (19th Century)
A Mortifying Mistake 104

Tom Prideaux (1908-   )
Skip-scoop-anellie 104

A. T. Quiller-Couch (1863-
1944)
Sage Counsel 104

Sir Walter Raleigh (1861-1922)
The Wishes of an Elderly
Man 105

William Brightly Rands (1823-
1882)
From Clean Clara 105

Laura E. Richards (1850-1943)
In Foreign Parts 106
The Shark 107

Mrs. Snipkin and Mrs.
   Wobblechin   107
Antonio   108

E. V. Rieu (1887-   )
Hall and Knight or
   z+b+x=y+b+z   108

James Whitcomb Riley (1849-
   1916)
The Man in the Moon   109

Emma Rounds (20th Century)
Johnny   110

Sir Owen Seaman (1861-1936)
The Uses of Ocean   110

James A. Sidey (19th Century)
The Irish Schoolmaster   111

L. de Giberne Sieveking
   (1896-   )
That'll Be All Right You'll
   Find   112
A Sad Case of Misapplied
   Concentration   112

William Jay Smith (1918-   )
The Floor and the Ceiling   113
The Toaster   114

G. N. Sprod (20th Century)
Request Number   114

George A. Strong (1832-1912)
The Modern Hiawatha   115

William Makepeace Thackeray
   (1811-1863)
A Tragic Story   115

Dylan Thomas (1914-1953)
From Under Milk Wood   115

Nancy Byrd Turner (1880-   )
Old Quin Queeribus   116

Carolyn Wells (1869-1942)
How to Tell the Wild
   Animals   116
A Tutor Who Tooted a
   Flute   117

Humbert Wolfe (1885-1940)
The Zoo   117

E. V. Wright (19th Century)
When Father Carves the
   Duck   118

T. R. Ybarra (1880-   )
Prose and Poesy: A Rural
   Misadventure   118

INTRODUCTION

THIS BOOK is full of the two best things in the world—laughter and poetry.

Most of us know about laughter, and let loose with cackles, guffaws, smiles, and giggles every now and then. But too few of us know, or even care, anything about poetry. One of the things I hope this book will do is to introduce you, with a smile, to poetry. The poetry in this book is light poetry, or "light verse," if you prefer. You can be sure that if you like this kind of poetry, you will also like all the other kinds of poetry. There is a whole world of it, and a wonderful world it is.

Most young people, especially boys, seem to be a little suspicious of poetry. For one thing, they're afraid that it is hard to read. They think they have to know the answer to "What is a sonnet?" or a pentameter, before they can begin to understand poetry. It isn't any mystery. You don't really have to know anything at all about the forms of poetry to start enjoying it. It doesn't really matter if a poem is a sonnet or a triolet or a double-dipped triphthong. If you like it, it's a good poem.

Sometimes, too, you are pushed too hard, and made to read difficult or serious poems before you have any feeling for poetry. It is hard to take joy in it when you're told to "memorize twenty lines for tomorrow," or to "describe in one hundred words the albatross's reactions upon first seeing the Ancient Mariner."

After you've soaked yourself in poetry for a while, you will easily learn what the poets are up to: what forms they are using, how they arrange the lines to hold your interest or to suit the words, the rhythms they use, and that kind of thing. But to start with, just relax, read what you like, and enjoy yourself.

Humorous poetry is a way of approaching serious poetry sideways. Once you become a poetry reader, you'll be one for life. And a head well stocked with poetry is the best kind of a head to have.

There are hundreds of good collections of poetry for young people in your library. But I haven't found one that collects humorous poetry only. Most of the books contain short sections called "Just For Fun," or "Jolly Poems." It is as though the person who put the book together said, "Oh, well . . . funny poems. They're not *really* important. I'll stick them in the back of the book where they won't get in the way of the serious stuff." When I was in school these funny sections were the most thumbed, marked, and appreciated parts of the books we used. I hope you will thumb, mark (within reason), and appreciate the poems in this book.

Nobody would expect you to like all of the poems in this book, or in any other book. A poem that makes one person fall on the floor with laughter might have no effect at all on the person next to him. You can show a friend a poem that you think is hysterically funny. He'll read it and mumble, "Umm, umm. . . . I see," looking as if he's at a funeral. Or if he's extra polite he may force a ghastly smile on his face and say, "Umm, umm, yes, yes. Very funny. Got any others?" This doesn't mean that he hasn't got a sense of humor, or that *you* haven't got a sense of humor. Your funnybones are adjusted differently. If he reads more humorous poetry, he'll find some that will set him laughing, and some that you will both laugh at.

Not many of the poems in this book were written especially for children. Most of them can also be found in collections of humor for adults. That is one of the nicest things about poetry—the oldsters can appreciate it just as much as the youngsters. It is a meeting-place, and will be enjoyed by both the parents and the children much more than any other kind of writing. Try it and see.

Just about half the poets in this book are Americans and half English. Everybody agrees, or almost everybody, that the best humorous poets who ever wrote were three Englishmen: Edward Lear, who is the King of Nonsense; W. S. Gilbert, who is the front half of Gilbert and Sullivan; and Lewis Carroll, the author of *Alice in Wonderland*. Carroll's other famous work is "The Hunting of the Snark." There is a shortened version of it in this book. The original is more than twice as long. You'll like it. It doesn't make a bit of sense.

Lear and Gilbert and Carroll are all old-timers. The modern light-verse artists most people like best are Ogden Nash, Morris Bishop, Hilaire Belloc, Arthur Guiterman, and Don Marquis. The Don Marquis poems about "archy" may look strange to you at first, but there's a reason. They were written by Mr. Marquis's friend archy the cockroach, in Mr. Marquis's newspaper office after the building was closed down for the night. Being a cockroach, archy had trouble working the typewriter, and couldn't make capital letters. He tells about his method in the poem on page 95.

Many of the best poems in this book were written by "serious" poets who, from time to time, would take off their black suits and put on polka dots. There is T. S. Eliot, who is considered by many the most serious poet in the world, and E. E. Cummings, A. E. Housman, John Keats, and Dylan Thomas.

The poems are arranged alphabetically by the author's names. Nobody knows (at least I don't) who wrote the poems in the first section of the book under the heading "Anonymous." Some books print these with "Author Unknown" under them, or with Anonymous's nickname, "Anon."

One last word: do not try to read all the poems in the book at one sitting. If you do, they will seem to get less funny as you go along. Humorous poems are like ice cream. One dish of ice cream tastes wonderful, and the second, and the third; but when you get to the tenth you begin to wonder if you really *do* like ice cream.

I hope you meet poetry here, shake hands with her, smile, and have her your friend for life.

I am grateful for the help and advice I received from many people while I was putting this book together, but I want to give particular thanks to five people—a mother, a teacher, a librarian, a bookseller, and a boy.

The mother in question is my wife, Peggy Bennett Cole, who did a lot of dreary typing, gave good advice, and laughed at the poems. The teacher is Abby Brown of Hunter High School in New York City, the librarian is Maria Cimino of the Children's Room of the New York Public Library, the bookseller is Carol Cox of New York, and the boy is Thomas Bissell of Rowayton, Connecticut, who read the poems and commented on them in the light of his three special qualifications: his good taste, his sense of humor, and his age.

WILLIAM COLE

HUMOROUS POETRY
FOR
CHILDREN

ANONYMOUS

TO BE OR NOT TO BE

I sometimes think I'd rather crow
And be a rooster than to roost
And be a crow. But I dunno.

A rooster he can roost also,
Which don't seem fair when crows
   can't crow.
Which may help some. Still I
   dunno.

Crows should be glad of one thing,
   though;
Nobody thinks of eating crow,
While roosters they are good enough
For anyone unless they're tough.

There are lots of tough old roosters,
   though,
And anyway a crow can't crow,
So mebby roosters stand more show.
It looks that way. But I dunno.

THE COMMON CORMORANT

The common cormorant or shag
Lays eggs inside a paper bag.
The reason you will see no doubt
It is to keep the lightning out.
But what these unobservant birds
Have never noticed is that herds
Of wandering bears may come with
   buns
And steal the bags to hold the
   crumbs.

RHYME FOR A SIMPLETON

I said, "This horse, sir, will you
   shoe?"
   And soon the horse was shod.
I said, "This deed, sir, will you do?"
   And soon the deed was dod!

I said, "This stick, sir, will you
   break?"
   At once the stick he broke.
I said, "This coat, sir, will you
   make?"
   And soon the coat he moke!

THE GROANING BOARD

A buttery, sugary, syrupy waffle—
Gee, but I love it somep'n awful.
Gingercakes dripping with choco-
   late goo,
Oo! How I love 'em! Oo! Oo! OO!
                   PINK

AFTER OLIVER

My sense of sight is very keen,
 My sense of hearing weak.
One time I saw a mountain pass,
 But could not hear its peak.
                OLIVER HERFORD

Why, Ollie, that you failed in this
 Is not so very queer,
To hear its peak you should, you
  know,
 Have had a mountaineer.
                BOSTON TRANSCRIPT

But if I saw a mountain pass,
 My eye I'd never drop;
I'd keep it turned upon the height,
 And see the mountain's top.
    PHILADELPHIA PUBLIC LEDGER

POOR OLD LADY

Poor old lady, she swallowed a fly.
I don't know why she swallowed a
  fly.
Poor old lady, I think she'll die.

Poor old lady, she swallowed a
  spider.
It squirmed and wriggled and turned
  inside her.
She swallowed the spider to catch
  the fly.
I don't know why, *etc.*

Poor old lady, she swallowed a bird.
How absurd! She swallowed a bird.
She swallowed the bird to catch the
  spider,
She swallowed the spider to catch
  the fly, *etc.*

Poor old lady, she swallowed a cat.
Think of that! She swallowed a cat.
She swallowed the cat to catch the
  bird.

She swallowed the bird to catch the
  spider, *etc.*

Poor old lady, she swallowed a dog.
She went the whole hog when she
  swallowed the dog.
She swallowed the dog to catch the
  cat.
She swallowed the cat to catch the
  bird, *etc.*

Poor old lady, she swallowed a cow.
I don't know how she swallowed the
  cow.
She swallowed the cow to catch the
  dog, *etc.*

Poor old lady, she swallowed a
  horse.
She died, of course.

GET UP, GET UP

Get up, get up, you lazy-head,
 Get up you lazy sinner,
We need those sheets for table-
  cloths,
 It's nearly time for dinner!

MR. FINNEY'S TURNIP

Mr. Finney had a turnip
 And it grew behind the barn;
And it grew and it grew,
 And that turnip did no harm.

There it grew and it grew
 Till it could grow no longer;
Then his daughter Lizzie picked it
 And put it in the cellar.

There it lay and it lay
 Till it began to rot;
And his daughter Suzie took it
 And put it in the pot.

And they boiled it and boiled it
 As long as they were able;

And then his daughters took it
And put it on the table.

Mr. Finney and his wife
They sat them down to sup;
And they ate and they ate
And they ate that turnip up.

AUNT MAUD

I had written to Aunt Maud
Who was on a trip abroad,
When I heard she'd died of cramp
Just too late to save the stamp.

AS I WAS STANDING IN THE STREET

As I was standing in the street,
As quiet as could be,
A great big ugly man came up
And tied his horse to me.

PEAS

I always eat peas with honey,
I've done it all my life,
They do taste kind of funny,
But it keeps them on the knife.

JAYBIRD

Jaybird a-sitting on a hickory limb;
He winked at me and I winked at
him.

I picked up a rock and hit him on
the chin.
Says he, "Young feller, don't you do
that again!"

OLD FARMER BUCK

Old Farmer Buck, he bought him a
duck
And he cut off her feet 'cause her
walked in the muck;
And when her wouldn't go for to
roost like a crow,
He cut off her head for to make her
do so.

Why does he go for to act this-a-
way?
Because he were a fool,
and a great big fool,
Because he were a fool,
as we all do say.

Old Farmer Bourne, he bought him
a horn
For to get him up early in the chill
of the morn;
And how did he know what time
for to blow?
He said he could tell by the rooster's
crow.

Why does he go for to act this-a-
way? etc.

Old Farmer Bunn, he bought him a
gun
And he looked down the barrel
for to see how 'twere done;
At the very first try it got him in the
eye
And he never had time for to say
good-by.

Why does he go for to act this-a-
way? etc.

OLD ENGLISH FOLK SONG

[23]

O I C

I'm in a 10der mood today
  & feel poetic, 2;
4 fun I'll just—off a line
  & send it off 2 U.

I'm sorry you've been 6 o long;
  Don't B disconsol8;
But bear your ills with 42de,
  & they won't seem so gr8.

THE PRODIGAL EGG

An egg of humble sphere
  By vain ambition stung,
Once left his mother dear
  When he was very young.

'Tis needless to dilate
  Upon a tale so sad;
The egg, I grieve to state,
  Grew very, very bad.

At last when old and blue,
  He wandered home, and then
They gently broke it to
  The loving mother hen.

She only said, in fun,
"I fear you're spoiled, my son!"

NIRVANA

I am
  A Clam!
Come learn of me
Unclouded peace and calm content,
  Serene, supreme tranquillity,
Where thoughtless dreams and
  dreamless thoughts are blent.

When the salt tide is rising to the
  flood,
  In billows blue my placid pulp I
  lave;
And when it ebbs I slumber in the
  mud,

Content alike with ooze or crystal
  wave.

I do not shudder when in chowder
  stewed,
Nor when the Coney Islander en-
  gulfs me raw.
When in the church soup's dreary
  solitude
Alone I wander, do I shudder?
  Naw!

If jarring tempests beat upon my
  bed,
  Or summer peace there be,
I do not care: as I have said,
  All's one to me;
    A Clam
    I am.

THE MICROBES

Two microbes sat on a pantry shelf
  And watched, with expressions
    pained,
  The milkmaid's stunts;
    And both said at once,
"Our relations are going to be
    strained."

AS I WAS LAYING ON THE GREEN

As I was laying on the green,
A small English book I seen.
Carlyle's *Essay on Burns* was the
  edition,

[24]

So I left it laying in the same position.

STATELY VERSE

If Mary goes far out to sea,
  By wayward breezes fanned,
I'd like to know—can you tell me?—
  Just where would Maryland?

If Tenny went high up in air
  And looked o'er land and lea,
Looked here and there and everywhere,
  Pray what would Tennessee?

I looked out of the window and
  Saw Orry on the lawn;
He's not there now, and who can tell
  Just where has Oregon?

Two girls were quarrelling one day
  With garden tools, and so
I said, "My dears, let Mary rake
  And just let Idaho."

A friend of mine lived in a flat
  With half a dozen boys;
When he fell ill I asked him why.
  He said: "I'm Illinois."

An English lady had a steed.
  She called him 'Ighland Bay.
She rode for exercise, and thus
  Rhode Island every day.

THE KILKENNY CATS

There wanst was two cats at Kilkenny,
Each thought there was one cat too
    many,
  So they quarrell'd and fit,
  They scratch'd and they bit,
  Till, excepting their nails,
  And the tips of their tails,
Instead of two cats, there warnt any.

I'M A LITTLE HINDOO

I'm a little Hindoo,
I do all I kindoo.
Where my pants and shirt don't
    meet
I make my little skindoo.

A CENTIPEDE WAS HAPPY QUITE

A centipede was happy quite,
  Until a frog in fun
Said, "Pray, which leg comes after
    which?"
This raised her mind to such a pitch,
She lay distracted in the ditch
  Considering how to run.

TAILS

De coon's got a long ringed bushy
tail,
De 'possum's tail is bare;
Dat rabbit hain't got no tail 'tall,
'Cep' a liddle bunch o' hair.

De gobbler's got a big fan tail,
De pattridge's tail is small;
Dat peacock's tail's got great big
eyes,
But dey don't see nothin' 'tall.

CONVERSATIONAL

"How's your father?" came the
whisper,
Bashful Ned the silence breaking;
"Oh, he's nicely," Annie murmured,
Smilingly the question taking.

Conversation flagged a moment,
Hopeless Ned essayed another:
"Annie, I—I," then a coughing,
And the question, "How's your
mother?"

"Mother? Oh, she's doing finely!"
Fleeting fast was all forbearance,
When in low, despairing accents,
Came the climax, "How's your
parents?"

BRIAN O'LINN

Brian O'Linn was a gentleman born,
His hair it was long and his beard
unshorn,
His teeth were out and his eyes far
in—
"I'm a wonderful beauty," says
Brian O'Linn!

Brian O'Linn was hard up for a coat,
He borrowed the skin of a neighbor-
ing goat,
He buckled the horns right under
his chin—
"They'll answer for pistols," says
Brian O'Linn!

Brian O'Linn had no breeches to wear,
He got him a sheepskin to make him a pair,
With the fleshy side out and the wooly side in—
"They are pleasant and cool," says Brian O'Linn!

Brian O'Linn had no hat to his head,
He stuck on a pot that was under the shed,
He murdered a cod for the sake of his fin—
"'Twill pass for a feather," says Brian O'Linn!

Brian O'Linn had no shirt to his back,
He went to a neighbor and borrowed a sack,
He puckered a meal-bag under his chin—
"They'll take it for ruffles," says Brian O'Linn!

Brian O'Linn had no shoes at all,
He bought an old pair at a cobbler's stall,
The uppers were broke and the soles were thin—
"They'll do me for dancing," says Brian O'Linn!

Brian O'Linn had no watch for to wear,
He bought a fine turnip and scooped it out fair,
He slipped a live cricket right under the skin—
"They'll think it is ticking," says Brian O'Linn!

Brian O'Linn was in want of a brooch,
He stuck a brass pin in a big cockroach,
The breast of his shirt he fixed it straight in—
"They'll think it's a diamond," says Brian O'Linn!

Brian O'Linn went a-courting one night,
He set both the mother and daughter to fight—
"Stop, stop," he exclaimed, "if you have but the tin,
I'll marry you both," says Brian O'Linn!

Brian O'Linn went to bring his wife home,
He had but one horse, that was all skin and bone—
"I'll put her behind me, as nate as a pin,
And her mother before me," says Brian O'Linn!

Brian O'Linn and his wife and wife's mother,
They all crossed over the bridge together,
The bridge broke down, and they all tumbled in—
"We'll go home by water," says Brian O'Linn!

Irish Street Ballad

RUMBO AND JUMBO

Lord Rumbo was immensely rich
And he would stick at nothing.
He went about in golden boots
And silver underclothing.

Lord Jumbo, on the other hand,
Though mentally acuter,
Could only run to silver boots,
His underclothes were pewter.

YOUNG SAMMY WATKINS

Young Sammy Watkins jumped out
     of bed;
   He ran to his sister and cut off her
     head.
This gave his dear mother a great
     deal of pain;
   She hopes that he never will do
     it again.

SISTER NELL

In the family drinking well
Willie pushed his sister Nell.
She's there yet, because it kilt her—
Now we have to buy a filter.

WILLIE THE POISONER

Willie poisoned Auntie's tea,
Auntie died in agony.
Uncle came and looked quite vexed,
"Really, Will," said he, "what next?"

CARELESS WILLIE

Willie, with a thirst for gore,
Nailed his sister to the door.

Mother said, with humor quaint:
"Now, Willie dear, don't scratch the
     paint."

LIMERICKS

An epicure, dining at Crewe,
Found quite a large mouse in his
     stew.
   Said the waiter, "Don't shout,
   And wave it about,
Or the rest will be wanting one, too!"

There was an old man from Antigua,
Whose wife said, "My dear, what a
     pig you are!"
   He replied, "O my queen,
   Is it manners you mean,
Or do you refer to my fig-u-a?"

A maiden caught stealing a dahlia,
Said, "Oh, you shan't tell on me,
     shahlia?"
   But the florist was hot,
   And he said, "Like as not
They'll send you to jail, you bad
     gahlia."

There was a young man so be-
     nighted,
He never knew when he was slighted.
   He went to a party,
   And ate just as hearty
As if he'd been really invited.

There was a young man of Herne
     Bay,
Who was making explosives one day;
   But he dropped his cigar

[28]

In the gunpowder jar.
There *was* a young man of Herne
  Bay.

A silly young fellow named Hyde
In a funeral procession was spied;
  When asked, "Who is dead?"
  He giggled and said,
"I don't know; I just came for the
  ride."

There was an old man of Tarentum,
Who gnashed his false teeth till he
  bent 'em.
  When they asked him the cost
  Of what he had lost,
He replied, "I can't say, for I rent
  'em."

There was an old person of Tring
Who, when somebody asked her to
  sing,
  Replied, "Isn't it odd?
  I can never tell *God
Save the Weasel* from *Pop Goes the
  King!*"

A decrepit old gasman, named Peter,
While hunting around for the meter,
  Touched a leak with his light;
  He rose out of sight—
And, as everyone who knows any-
  thing about poetry can tell you,
  he also ruined the meter.

A flea and a fly in a flue
Were imprisoned, so what could
  they do?
  Said the fly, "Let us flee,"
  Said the flea, "Let us fly,"
So they flew through a flaw in the
  flue.

A boy who played tunes on a comb,
Had become such a nuisance at
  homb,
  That ma spanked him, and then—
  "Will you do it again?"
And he cheerfully answered her,
  "Nomb."

There was an old man of Blackheath,
Who sat on his set of false teeth.
  Said he, with a start,
  "O Lord, bless my heart!
I've bitten myself underneath!"

❖❖❖

FRANKLIN P. ADAMS

THE RICH MAN

The rich man has his motorcar,
  His country and his town estate.
He smokes a fifty-cent cigar
  And jeers at Fate.

He frivols through the livelong day,
  He knows not Poverty, her pinch.
His lot seems light, his heart seems
  gay;
  He has a cinch.

Yet though my lamp burns low and
    dim,
Though I must slave for liveli-
    hood—
Think you that I would change with
    him?
    You bet I would!

◇◇◇

DOROTHY ALDIS

BLUM

Dog means dog,
And cat means cat;
And there are lots
Of words like that.

A cart's a cart
To pull or shove,
A plate's a plate,
To eat off of.

But there are other
Words I say
When I am left
Alone to play.

Blum is one.
Blum is a word
That very few
Have ever heard.

I like to say it,
"Blum, Blum, Blum"—
I do it loud
Or in a hum.

All by itself
It's nice to sing:
It does not mean
A single thing.

OUR SILLY LITTLE SISTER

To begin with she wouldn't have
    fallen in

If she hadn't been acting so silly.
First thing we saw was her hair rib-
    bon there
On top like a water lily.

In less than a minute we'd gotten
    her out
And set her down quickly to drain,
And do you know what she said
    through her dripping hair?
"I want to go swimming again."

"Swimming?" we cried. "Do you
    think *you* can swim?"
She sat there so scowly and black.
*"Much better than you can, besides
    I don't care!"*
We couldn't think what to say back.

◇◇◇

N. P. BABCOCK

THE STRANGER CAT

A little girl with golden hair
Was rocking in her grandma's chair,
When in there walked a Stranger
    Cat.
(I'm *sure* there's nothing strange in
    that.)

It was a cat with kinky ears
And very aged for its years.
The little girl remarked "O scat!"
(I *think* there's nothing strange in
    that.)

But presently with stealthy tread
The Cat, which at her word had fled,
Returned with cane, and boots and
    hat.
(I *fear* there's something strange in
    that.)

"Excuse me," and the cat bowed
 low,
"I hate to trouble you, you know,
But tell me, have you seen a rat?"
(I *know* there's something strange
 in that.)

The little girl was very shy—
"Well, really I can't say that I
Have seen one lately, Mr. Cat."
(I'm *sure* there's something strange
 in that.)

"Oh, haven't you?" the Cat replied;
"Thanks, I am deeply gratified.
I really couldn't eat a rat."
(We *all* know what to think of
 that.)

And then the cat with kinky ears
And so much wisdom for its years
Retired, with a soft pit-a-pat
(And that was all there was of that).

◇◇◇

HILAIRE BELLOC

THE YAK

As a friend to the children commend
 me the yak.
You will find it exactly the thing:

It will carry and fetch, you can ride
 on its back,
Or lead it about with a string.

A Tartar who dwells on the plains
 of Thibet
(A desolate region of snow)
Has for centuries made it a nursery
 pet,
And surely the Tartar should
 know!

Then tell your papa where the Yak
 can be got,
And if he is awfully rich,
He will buy you the creature—or
 else he will *not*.
(I cannot be positive which.)

G

stands for Gnu, whose weapons of
 Defence
Are long, sharp, curling Horns, and
 Common-sense,

To these he adds a Name so short
 and strong,
That even Hardy Boers pronounce
 it wrong.
How often on a bright Autumnal
 day
The Pious people of Pretoria say,
"Come, let us hunt the——" Then
 no more is heard

[31]

But Sounds of Strong Men strug-
gling with a word.
Meanwhile, the distant Gnu with
grateful eyes
Observes his opportunity, and flies.

Child, if you have a rummy kind of
name,
Remember to be thankful for the
same.

THE FROG

Be kind and tender to the Frog,
  And do not call him names,
As "Slimy-Skin," or "Polly-wog,"
  Or likewise, "Ugly James,"
Or "Gape-a-grin," or "Toad-gone-
    wrong,"
  Or "Billy-Bandy-knees";
The Frog is justly sensitive
  To epithets like these.

No animal will more repay
  A treatment kind and fair,
At least, so lonely people say
Who keep a frog (and, by the way,
  They are extremely rare).

THE HIPPOPOTAMUS

I shoot the Hippopotamus
With bullets made of platinum,
Because if I use leaden ones
His hide is sure to flatten 'em.

GEORGE,

*Who played with a Dangerous Toy,
and suffered a Catastrophe of con-
siderable Dimensions.*

When George's Grandmamma was
    told

That George had been as good as
    Gold,
She Promised in the Afternoon
To buy him an *Immense* BAL-
    LOON.
And
    so she did; but when it came,
It got into the candle flame,
And being of a dangerous sort
Exploded
    with a loud report!
The Lights went out! The Windows
    broke!
The Room was filled with reeking
    smoke.
And in the darkness shrieks and yells
Were mingled with Electric Bells,
And falling masonry and groans,
And crunching, as of broken bones,
And dreadful shrieks, when, worst
    of all,
The House itself began to fall!
It tottered, shuddering to and fro,
Then crashed into the street below—
Which happened to be Savile Row.

        .   .   .   .   .
When Help arrived, among the Dead
Were
    Cousin Mary,
      Little Fred,
The Footman
    (both of them),
      The Groom,
The man that cleaned the Billiard-
    Room,
The Chaplain, and
      The Still-Room Maid.
And I am dreadfully afraid
That Monsieur Champignon, the
    Chef,
Will now be
      permanently deaf—
And both his

Aides
  are much the same;
While George, who was in part to
    blame,
Received, you will regret to hear,
A nasty lump
  behind the ear.

MORAL

The moral is that little Boys
Should not be given dangerous Toys.

❖❖❖

JOHN BENNETT

A TIGER'S TALE

There was an ancient Grecian boy
Who played upon the fiddle,
Sometimes high, sometimes low,
Sometimes in the middle;
And all day long beneath the shade
He lunched on prunes and marma-
    lade;
But what the tunes were which he
    played
  Is certainly a riddle.

Three tigers, gaunt and ravenous,

Came from the gloomy wood,
Intent to slay the fiddler,
But his music was too good;
So round about him once they filed,
Till by the melody beguiled,
They sat them softly down and
    smiled,
  As only tigers could.

And thus beguiled, the tigers smiled
Throughout the livelong day
Until, at length, there was not left
  Another tune to play.

What happened then I do not know
I was not there to see.
But when a man runs short on
    tunes,
Can tigers be appeased with prunes,
Or marmalade and silver spoons?
  That's what perplexes me.

❖❖❖

MORRIS BISHOP

SONG OF THE POP-BOTTLERS

Pop bottles pop-bottles
  In pop shops;

[33]

The pop-bottles Pop bottles
  Poor Pop drops.

When Pop drops pop-bottles,
  Pop-bottles plop!
Pop-bottle-tops topple!
  Pop mops slop!

Stop! Pop'll drop bottle!
  Stop, Pop, stop!
When Pop bottles pop-bottles,
  Pop-bottles pop!

OZYMANDIAS REVISITED

I met a traveller from an antique
land

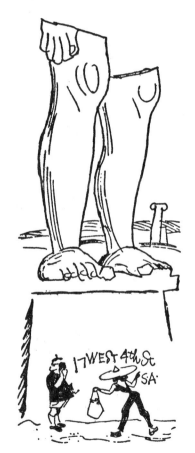

Who said: Two vast and trunkless
  legs of stone
Stand in the desert. Near them on
  the sand,
Half sunk, a shatter'd visage lies,
  whose frown
And wrinkled lip and sneer of cold
  command
Tell that its sculptor well those pas-
  sions read
Which yet survive, stamp'd on these
  lifeless things,
The hand that mocked them and
  the heart that fed;
And on the pedestal these words
  appear:
"My name is Ozymandias, king of
  kings!
Look on my works, ye Mighty, and
  despair!"
Also the names of Emory P. Gray,
Mr. and Mrs. Dukes, and Oscar
  Baer,
Of 17 West 4th Street, Oyster Bay.

THE TALES THE BARBERS
TELL

After the day is over
  And the passers-by are rare
The lights burn low in the barber-
  shop
  And the shades are drawn with
  care
To hide the haughty barbers
  Cutting each other's hair.

And dreadful tales they whisper
  To the music of the shears,
How even the deftest razor slips
  And cleaves the client's ears;
And here is the dreadfullest story
  The seated barber hears:

"A customer came to the Parlor
  And sank in the barber's chair
As a tired child sinks in his mother's
    arms
  And rests and huddles there;
His beard was lank and tangled,
  And burrs were in his hair.

" 'A shave!' I heard him mutter
  In accents soft and low;
I shaved him twice; and then I said,
  'A hair-cut, sir, also?'
A red-hot towel enswathed him,
  He could not answer no.

"I used the shears and clippers,
  The whisk and air-blast too,
And then I whispered in his ear:
  'Excuse me, sir, but you
Urgently need our Special
  Egg Gasoline Shampoo.'

"I think I heard him murmur,
  I think that he agreed;
I soaped and beat and ground his
    head
  Till it began to bleed;
'A face massage?' His silence
  Signified, 'Proceed!'

"I cured his hair of dandruff
  With all the cures there are,
I rubbed his scalp with alcohol,
  I scrubbed his face with tar,
I singed his hair and dressed it
  With oil and vinegar.

"All of my art I lavished
  On that unworthy head;
'Rise up, rise up, go kingly forth,
  For I have done!' I said.
But never a word he answered;
  My customer was dead!"

This is the dreadful story
  That barber tells whene'er

The shades are drawn in the barber-
    shop
  And the midnight Mazdas flare
On the hushed and haughty barbers
  Cutting each other's hair.

❖❖❖

ISAAC H. BROMLEY

THE PASSENJARE

The conductor when he receives a
    fare,
Must punch in the presence of the
    passenjare;
  A blue trip slip for a 8-cent fare,
  A buff trip slip for a 6-cent fare,
  A pink trip slip for a 3-cent fare,
All in the presence of the passenjare.
Punch, boys, punch, punch with ·
    care,
All in the presence of the passenjare.

❖❖❖

B. CURTIS BROWN

JONATHAN BING

Poor old Jonathan Bing
Went out in his carriage to visit the
    King,
But everyone pointed and said,
    "Look at that!
Jonathan Bing has forgotten his
    hat!"
(He'd forgotten his hat!)

Poor old Jonathan Bing
Went home and put on a new hat
    for the King,
But up by the palace a soldier said,
    "Hi!
You can't see the King; you've for-

[35]

gotten your tie!"
(He'd forgotten his tie!)

Poor old Jonathan Bing,
He put on a beautiful tie for the
King,
But when he arrived an Archbishop
said, "Ho!
You can't come to court in pajamas,
you know!"

Poor old Jonathan Bing
Went home and addressed a short
note to the King:
"If you please will excuse me I won't
come to tea,
For home's the best place for all
people like me!"

◇◇◇

GELETT BURGESS

I WISH THAT MY ROOM HAD A FLOOR

I wish that my room had a floor;
I don't so much care for a door,
But this walking around
Without touching the ground
Is getting to be such a bore.

THE PURPLE COW

I never saw a Purple Cow,
I never hope to see one,
But I can tell you, anyhow,
I'd rather see than be one!

TRICKY

I seen a dunce of a poet once, a-
writin' a little book;
And he says to me with a smile, says
he, "Here's a pome—d' you want
to look?"

And I threw me eye at the pome;
say I, "What's the use o' this here
rot?"
"It's a double sestine," says he, look-
in' mean, "and they're hard as the
deuce, that's what!"

◇◇◇

W. A. BUTLER

TOM TWIST

Tom Twist was a wonderful fellow,
No boy was so nimble and strong;
He could turn ten somersets back-
ward,
And stand on his head all day
long.
No wrestling, or leaping, or running
This tough little urchin could tire;
His muscles were all gutta-percha,
And his sinews bundles of wire.

Tom Twist liked the life of a sailor,
So off, with a hop and a skip,
He went to a Nantucket captain,
Who took him on board of his
ship.
The vessel was crowded with sea-
men,
Young, old, stout and slim, short
and tall,
But in climbing, swinging, and
jumping,
Tom Twist was ahead of them all.

He could scamper all through the
rigging,
As spry and as still as a cat,
While as to a leap from the maintop
To deck, he thought nothing of
that:
He danced at the end of the yard-
arm,

[36]

Slept sound in the bend of a sail,
And hung by his legs from the bowsprit,
When the wind was blowing a
gale.

The vessel went down in a tempest,
A thousand fathoms or more;
And Tom Twist dived under the
breakers,
And, swimming five miles, got
ashore.
The shore was a cannibal island,
The natives were hungry enough;
But they felt of Tommy all over,
And found him entirely too tough.

So they put him into a boy-coop—
Just to fatten him up, you see—
But Tommy crept out, very slowly,
And climbed to the top of a tree.
The tree was the nest of a condor,
A bird with prodigious big wings,
Which lived upon boa constrictors
And other digestible things.

The condor flew home in the evening,
And there lay friend Tommy so
snug,
She thought she had pounced on a
very
Remarkable species of bug;
She soon woke him up with her
pecking,
But Tommy gave one of his
springs,
And leaped on the back of the
condor,
Between her long neck and her
wings.

The condor tried plunging and
pitching,

But Tommy held on with firm
hand,
Then off, with a scream, flew the
condor,
O'er forest and ocean and land.
By and by she got tired of her
burden,
And flying quite close to the
ground,
Tom untwisted his legs from the
creature,
And quickly slipped off with a
bound.

He landed all right, and feet fore-
most,
A little confused by his fall,
And then ascertained he had lighted
On top of the great Chinese Wall.
He walked to the city of Pekin,
Where he made the Chinamen
grin;
He turned ten somersets backward,
And they made him a Mandarin.

Then he sailed for his dear home
and harbor.
The house of his mother he knew;
He climbed up the lightning rod
quickly,
And came down the chimney flue.
His mother in slumber lay dreaming
That she never would see him
more,
When she opened her eyes, and
Tommy
Stood there on the bedroom floor!

Her nightcap flew off in amazement,
Her hair stood on end with sur-
prise.
"What kind of a ghost or a spirit
Is this that I see with my eyes?"

[37]

"I am your most dutiful Tommy."
"I will not believe it," she said,
"Till you turn ten somersets back-
ward,
And stand half an hour on your
head."
"That thing I will do, dearest
mother."
At once with a skip and a hop,
He turned ten somersets backward,
But then was unable to stop!
The tenth took him out of the
window,
His mother jumped from her bed,
To see his twentieth somerset
Take him over the kitchen shed;

Thence, across the patch of potatoes,
And beyond the church on the
hill;
She saw him tumbling and turning,
Turning and tumbling still—
Till Tommy's body diminished
In size to the head of a pin,
Spinning away in the distance,
Where it still continues to spin!

◇◇◇

C. S. CALVERLEY

LOVE

Canst thou love me, lady?
I've not learn'd to woo;
Thou art on the shady
Side of sixty, too.
Still I love thee dearly!
Thou hast lands and pelf:
But I love thee merely
Merely for thyself.

Wilt thou love me, fairest?
Though thou art not fair;
And I think thou wearest

Someone else's hair.
Thou could'st love, though, dearly;
And, as I am told,
Thou art very nearly
Worth thy weight in gold.

Dost thou love me, sweet one?
Tell me that thou dost!
Women fairly beat one
But I think thou must.
Thou art loved so dearly:
I am plain, but then
Thou (to speak sincerely)
Art as plain again.

Love me, bashful fairy!
I've an empty purse:
And I've "moods," which vary;
Mostly for the worst.
Still, I love thee dearly:
Though I make (I feel)
Love a little queerly,
I'm as true as steel.

Love me, swear to love me
(As you know, they do)
By yon heaven above me
And its changeless blue.
Love me, lady, dearly,
If you'll be so good;
Though I don't see clearly
On what ground you should.

Love me—ah! or love me
Not, but be my bride!
Do not simply shove me
(So to speak) aside!
P'raps it would be dearly
Purchased at the price;
But a hundred yearly
Would be very nice.

From MORNING

When the ploughman, as he goes
Leathern-gaitered o'er the snows,

[38]

From his hat and from his nose
  Knocks the ice;
And the panes are frosted o'er
And the lawn is crisp and hoar,
  As has been observed before
  Once or twice.

When arrayed in breastplate red
Sings the robin, for his bread,
On the elm tree that hath shed
  Every leaf;
While, within, the frost benumbs
The still sleepy schoolboy's thumbs,
And in consequence his sums
  Come to grief.

But when breakfast-time hath come,
And he's crunching crust and crumb,
He'll no longer look a glum
  Little dunce;
But be brisk as bees that settle
On a summer rose's petal:
Wherefore, Polly, put the kettle
  On at once.

◇◇◇

LEWIS CARROLL

FATHER WILLIAM

"You are old, Father William," the
  young man said,
  "And your hair has become very
  white;
And yet you incessantly stand on
  your head—
  Do you think, at your age, it is
  right?"

"In my youth," Father William replied to his son,
  "I feared it might injure the brain;
But now that I'm perfectly sure I
  have none,

Why, I do it again and again."

"You are old," said the youth, "as I
  mentioned before,
  And have grown most uncommonly fat;
Yet you turned a back-somersault in
  at the door—
  Pray, what is the reason of that?"

"In my youth," said the sage, as he
  shook his gray locks,
  "I kept all my limbs very supple
By the use of this ointment—one
  shilling the box—
  Allow me to sell you a couple?"

"You are old," said the youth, "and
  your jaws are too weak
  For anything tougher than suet;
Yet you finished the goose, with the
  bones and the beak—
  Pray, how did you manage to do
  it?"

"In my youth," said his father, "I
  took to the law,
  And argued each case with my
  wife;
And the muscular strength which it
  gave to my jaw
  Has lasted the rest of my life."

"You are old," said the youth; "one
  would hardly suppose
  That your eye was as steady as
  ever;
Yet you balanced an eel on the end
  of your nose—
  What made you so awfully
  clever?"

"I have answered three questions,
  and that is enough,"
  Said his father, "don't give yourself airs!

Do you think I can listen all day to
    such stuff?
Be off, or I'll kick you downstairs!"

HE THOUGHT HE SAW

He thought he saw an Elephant,
    That practised on a fife:
He looked again, and found it was
    A letter from his wife.
"At length I realise," he said,
    "The bitterness of Life!"

He thought he saw a Buffalo
    Upon the chimney piece:
He looked again, and found it was
    His Sister's Husband's Niece.
"Unless you leave this house," he
        said,
    "I'll send for the Police!"

He thought he saw a Rattlesnake
    That questioned him in Greek:
He looked again, and found it was
    The Middle of Next Week.
"The one thing I regret," he said,
    "Is that it cannot speak!"

He thought he saw a Banker's Clerk
    Descending from the bus:
He looked again, and found it was
    A Hippopotamus:
"If this should stay to dine," he said,
    "There won't be much for us!"

He thought he saw an Albatross
    That fluttered round the lamp:
He looked again, and found it was
    A Penny-Postage-Stamp.
"You'd best be getting home," he
        said;
    "The nights are very damp!"

He thought he saw a Coach-and-
        Four
    That stood beside his bed:

He looked again, and found it was
    A Bear without a Head.
"Poor thing," he said, "poor silly
        thing!
    It's waiting to be fed!"

He thought he saw a Kangaroo
    That worked a coffee-mill:
He looked again, and found it was
    A Vegetable-Pill.
"Were I to swallow this," he said,
    "I should be very ill!"

THE WALRUS AND THE
CARPENTER

The sun was shining on the sea,
    Shining with all his might:
He did his very best to make
    The billows smooth and bright—
And this was odd, because it was
    The middle of the night.

The moon was shining sulkily,
    Because she thought the sun
Had got no business to be there
    After the day was done—
"It's very rude of him," she said,
    "To come and spoil the fun!"

The sea was wet as wet could be,
    The sands were dry as dry.
You could not see a cloud, because
    No cloud was in the sky:
No birds were flying overhead—
    There were no birds to fly.

The Walrus and the Carpenter
    Were walking close at hand:
They wept like anything to see
    Such quantities of sand.
"If this were only cleared away,"
    They said, "it *would* be grand!"

"If seven maids with seven mops
    Swept it for half a year,

Do you suppose," the Walrus said,
  "That they could get it clear?"
"I doubt it," said the Carpenter,
  And shed a bitter tear.

"O Oysters, come and walk with us!"
  The Walrus did beseech.
"A pleasant talk, a pleasant walk,
  Along the briny beach:
We cannot do with more than four,
  To give a hand to each."

The eldest Oyster looked at him,
  But never a word he said:
The eldest Oyster winked his eye,
  And shook his heavy head—
Meaning to say he did not choose
  To leave the oyster bed.

But four young Oysters hurried up,
  All eager for the treat:
Their coats were brushed, their
    faces washed,
  Their shoes were clean and neat—
And this was odd, because, you
    know,
  They hadn't any feet.

Four other Oysters followed them,
  And yet another four;
And thick and fast they came at last,
  And more, and more, and more—
All hopping through the frothy
    waves,
  And scrambling to the shore.

The Walrus and the Carpenter
  Walked on a mile or so,
And then they rested on a rock
  Conveniently low:
And all the little Oysters stood
  And waited in a row.

"The time has come," the Walrus
    said,
  "To talk of many things:

Of shoes and ships and sealing wax,
  Of cabbages and kings;
And why the sea is boiling hot—
  And whether pigs have wings."

"But wait a bit," the Oysters cried,
  "Before we have our chat;
For some of us are out of breath,
  And all of us are fat!"
"No hurry!" said the Carpenter.
  They thanked him much for that.

"A loaf of bread," the Walrus said,
  "Is what we chiefly need:
Pepper and vinegar besides
  Are very good indeed—
Now, if you're ready, Oysters dear,
  We can begin to feed."

"But not on us!" the Oysters cried,
  Turning a little blue.
"After such kindness, that would be
  A dismal thing to do!"
"The night is fine," the Walrus said.
  "Do you admire the view?"

"It was so kind of you to come!
  And you are very nice!"
The Carpenter said nothing but
  "Cut us another slice.
I wish you were not quite so deaf—
  I've had to ask you twice!"

"It seems a shame," the Walrus said,
  "To play them such a trick,
After we've brought them out so far,
  And made them trot so quick!"
The Carpenter said nothing but
  "The butter's spread too thick!"

"I weep for you," the Walrus said:
  "I deeply sympathize."
With sobs and tears he sorted out
  Those of the largest size,
Holding his pocket handkerchief
  Before his streaming eyes.

"O Oysters," said the Carpenter,
    "You've had a pleasant run!
Shall we be trotting home again?"
    But answer came there none—
And this was scarcely odd, because
    They'd eaten every one.

WAYS AND MEANS

I'll tell thee everything I can;
    There's little to relate.
I saw an aged aged man,
    A-sitting on a gate.
"Who are you, aged man?" I said,
    "And how is it you live?"
His answer trickled through my
        head
    Like water through a sieve.

He said, "I look for butterflies
    That sleep among the wheat:
I make them into mutton pies,
    And sell them in the street.
I sell them unto men," he said,
    "Who sail on stormy seas;
And that's the way I get my bread—
    A trifle, if you please."

But I was thinking of a plan
    To dye one's whiskers green,
And always use so large a fan
    That they could not be seen.
So, having no reply to give
    To what the old man said,
I cried, "Come, tell me how you
        live!"
    And thumped him on the head.

His accents mild took up the tale;
    He said, "I go my ways
And when I find a mountain rill
    I set it in a blaze;
And thence they make a stuff they
        call
    Rowland's Macassar Oil—

Yet twopence-halfpenny is all
    They give me for my toil."

But I was thinking of a way
    To feed oneself on batter,
And so go on from day to day
    Getting a little fatter.
I shook him well from side to side,
    Until his face was blue;
"Come, tell me how you live," I
        cried,
    "And what it is you do!"

He said, "I hunt for haddock's eyes
    Among the heather bright,
And work them into waistcoat
        buttons
    In the silent night.
And these I do not sell for gold
    Or coin of silvery shine,
But for a copper halfpenny
    And that will purchase nine.

"I sometimes dig for buttered rolls,
    Or set limed twigs for crabs;
I sometimes search the grassy knolls
    For wheels of Hansom cabs.
And that's the way" (he gave a
        wink)
    "By which I get my wealth—
And very gladly will I drink
    Your Honor's noble health."

I heard him then, for I had just
    Completed my design
To keep the Menai Bridge from rust
    By boiling it in wine.
I thanked him much for telling me
    The way he got his wealth,
But chiefly for his wish that he
    Might drink my noble health.

And now if e'er by chance I put
    My fingers into glue,
Or madly squeeze a right-hand foot
    Into a left-hand shoe,

[42]

Or if I drop upon my toe
  A very heavy weight,
I weep, for it reminds me so
Of that old man I used to know—
Whose look was mild, whose speech
  was slow,
Whose hair was whiter than the
  snow,
Whose face was very like a crow,
With eyes, like cinders, all aglow,
Who seemed distracted with his
  woe,
Who rocked his body to and fro,
And muttered mumblingly, and low,
As if his mouth were full of dough,
Who snorted like a buffalo—
That summer evening, long ago,
  A-sitting on a gate.

From THE HUNTING OF THE SNARK

"Just the place for a Snark!" the
  Bellman cried,
  As he landed his crew with care;
Supporting each man on the top of
  the tide
  By a finger entwined in his hair.

"Just the place for a Snark! I have
  said it twice:
  That alone should encourage the
  crew.
Just the place for a Snark! I have
  said it thrice:
  What I tell you three times is
  true."

The crew was complete: it included
  a Boots—
A maker of Bonnets and Hoods—
A Barrister, brought to arrange their
  disputes—
  And a Broker, to value their goods.

A Billiard-marker, whose skill was
  immense,
  Might perhaps have won more
  than his share—
But a Banker, engaged at enormous
  expense,
  Had the whole of their cash in his
  care.

There was also a Beaver, that paced
  on the deck,
  Or would sit making lace in the
  bow:
And had often (the Bellman said)
  saved them from wreck,
  Though none of the sailors knew
  how.

There was one who was famed for
  the number of things
  He forgot when he entered the
  ship:
His umbrella, his watch, all his
  jewels and rings,
  And the clothes he had bought
  for the trip.

He had forty-two boxes, all carefully
  packed,
  With his name painted clearly on
  each:
But, since he omitted to mention
  the fact,
  They were all left behind on the
  beach.

The loss of his clothes hardly mattered, because
  He had seven coats on when he
  came,
With three pairs of boots—but the
  worst of it was,
  He had wholly forgotten his name.

He would answer to "Hi!" or to any
  loud cry,

[43]

Such as "Fry me!" or "Fritter my
    wig!"
To "What-you-may-call-um!" or
    "What-was-his-name!"
But especially "Thing-um-a-jig!"

While, for those who preferred a
    more forcible word,
He had different names from
    these:
His intimate friends called him
    "Candle-ends,"
And his enemies "Toasted-
    cheese."

"His form is ungainly—his intellect
    small—"
    (So the Bellman would often
    remark)
"But his courage is perfect! And
    that, after all,
Is the thing that one needs with
    a Snark."

*   *   *

The Bellman himself they all praised
    to the skies—
Such a carriage, such ease and
    such grace!
Such solemnity, too! One could see
    he was wise,
The moment one looked in his
    face!

He had bought a large map repre-
    senting the sea,
Without the least vestige of land:
And the crew were much pleased
    when they found it to be
A map they could all understand.

"What's the good of Mercator's
    North Poles and Equators,
Tropics, Zones, and Meridian
    Lines?"

So the Bellman would cry: and the
    crew would reply
"They are merely conventional
    signs!

"Other maps are such shapes, with
    their islands and capes!
But we've got our brave Captain
    to thank"
(So the crew would protest) "that
    he's bought us the best—
A perfect and absolute blank!"

This was charming, no doubt: but
    they shortly found out
That the Captain they trusted so
    well
Had only one notion for crossing the
    ocean,
And that was to tingle his bell.

He was thoughtful and grave—but
    the orders he gave
Were enough to bewilder a crew.
When he cried "Steer to starboard,
    but keep her head larboard!"
What on earth was the helmsman
    to do?

Then the bowsprit got mixed with
    the rudder sometimes
A thing, as the Bellman remarked,
That frequently happens in tropical
    climes,
When a vessel is, so to speak,
    "snarked."

But the principal failing occurred in
    the sailing,
And the Bellman, perplexed and
    distressed,
Said he *had* hoped, at least, when
    the wind blew due East,
That the ship would *not* travel
    due West!

[44]

But the danger had passed—they
  had landed at last,
With their boxes, portmanteaus,
  and bags:
Yet at first sight the crew were not
  pleased with the view
Which consisted of chasms and
  crags.

The Bellman perceived that their
  spirits were low,
And repeated in musical tone
Some jokes he had kept for a season
  of woe—
But the crew would do nothing
  but groan.

      *   *   *

"We have sailed many months, we
  have sailed many weeks,
(Four weeks to the month you
  may mark),
But never as yet ('tis your Captain
  who speaks)
Have we caught the least glimpse
  of a Snark!

"We have sailed many weeks, we
  have sailed many days,
(Seven days to the week I allow),
But a Snark, on the which we might
  lovingly gaze,
We have never beheld till now!

"Come, listen, my men, while I tell
  you again
The five unmistakable marks
By which you may know, whereso-
  ever you go,
The warranted genuine Snarks.

"Let us take them in order. The first
  is the taste,
Which is meager and hollow, but
  crisp:

Like a coat that is rather too tight
  in the waist,
With a flavor of Will-o-the-wisp.

"Its habit of getting up late you'll
  agree
That it carries too far, when I say
That it frequently breakfasts at five
  o'clock tea,
And dines on the following day.

"The third is its slowness in taking
  a jest.
Should you happen to venture on
  one,
It will sigh like a thing that is deeply
  distressed:
And it always looks grave at a pun.

"The fourth is its fondness for bath-
  ing machines,
Which it constantly carries about,
And believes that they add to the
  beauty of scenes—
A sentiment open to doubt.

"The fifth is ambition. It next will
  be right
To describe each particular batch:
Distinguishing those that have
  feathers, and bite,
From those that have whiskers,
  and scratch.

"For, although common Snarks do
  no manner of harm,
Yet I feel it my duty to say
Some are Boojums—" The Bellman
  broke off in alarm,
For the Baker had fainted away.

They roused him with muffins—they
  roused him with ice—
They roused him with mustard
  and cress—
They roused him with jam and judi-
  cious advice—

[45]

They set him conundrums to
    guess.

When at length he sat up and was
    able to speak,
His sad story he offered to tell;
And the Bellman cried "Silence! Not
    even a shriek!"
And excitedly tingled his bell.

There was silence supreme! Not a
    shriek, not a scream,
Scarcely even a howl or a groan,
As the man they called "Ho!" told
    his story of woe
In an antediluvian tone.

"My father and mother were honest,
    though poor—"
"Skip all that!" cried the Bellman
    in haste,
'If it once becomes dark, there's no
    chance of a Snark,
We have hardly a minute to
    waste!"

"I skip forty years," said the Baker,
    in tears,
"And proceed without further
    remark
To the day when you took me aboard
    of your ship
To help you in hunting the Snark.

"A dear uncle of mine (after whom
    I was named)
Remarked, when I bade him fare-
    well—"
"Oh, skip your dear uncle," the Bell-
    man exclaimed,
As he angrily tingled his bell.

"He remarked to me then," said that
    mildest of men,
" 'If your Snark be a Snark, that
    is right;

Fetch it home by all means—you
    may serve it with greens
And it's handy for striking a light.

" 'You may seek it with thimbles—
    and seek it with care;
You may hunt it with forks and
    hope;
You may threaten its life with a rail-
    way share;
You may charm it with smiles and
    soap—

("That's exactly the method," the
    Bellman bold
In a hasty parenthesis cried,
"That's exactly the way I have al-
    ways been told
That the capture of Snarks should
    be tried!")

" 'But oh, beamish nephew, beware
    of the day,
If your Snark be a Boojum! For
    then
You will softly and suddenly vanish
    away,
And never be met with again!'

"It is this, it is this that oppresses
    my soul,
When I think of my uncle's last
    words;
And my heart is like nothing so
    much as a bowl
Brimming over with quivering
    curds!

"It is this, it is this—" "We have
    had that before!"
The Bellman indignantly said.
And the Baker replied, "Let me say
    it once more.
It is this, it is this, that I dread!

"I engage with the Snark—every
   night after dark—
In a dreamy delirious fight:
I serve it with greens in those
   shadowy scenes,
And I use it for striking a light:

"But if ever I meet with a Boojum,
   that day,
In a moment (of this I am sure),
I shall softly and suddenly vanish
   away—
And the notion I cannot endure!"

* * *

They sought it with thimbles, they
   sought it with care;
They pursued it with forks and
   hope;
They threatened its life with a rail-
   way share;
They charmed it with smiles and
   soap.

They shuddered to think that the
   chase might fail,
And the Beaver, excited at last,
Went bounding along on the tip of
   its tail,
For the daylight was nearly past.

"There is Thingumbob shouting!"
   the Bellman said.
"He is shouting like mad, only
   hark
He is waving his hands, he is wag-
   ging his head,
He has certainly found a Snark!"

They gazed in delight, while the
   Butcher exclaimed
"He was always a desperate wag!"
They beheld him—their Baker—
   their hero unnamed—

On the top of a neighboring crag,

Erect and sublime, for one moment
   of time,
In the next, that wild figure they
   saw
(As if stung by a spasm) plunge
   into a chasm,
While they waited and listened
   in awe.

"It's a Snark!" was the sound that
   first came to their ears,
And seemed almost too good to
   be true.
Then followed a torrent of laughter
   and cheers:
Then the ominous words "It's a
   Boo—"

Then, silence. Some fancied they
   heard in the air
A weary and wandering sigh
That sounded like "—jum!" but the
   others declare
It was only a breeze that went by.

They hunted till darkness came on,
   but they found
Not a button, or feather, or mark,
By which they could tell that they
   stood on the ground
Where the Baker had met with
   the Snark.

In the midst of the word he was
   trying to say,
In the midst of his laughter and
   glee,
He had softly and suddenly vanished
   away—
For the Snark *was* a Boojum, you
   see.

[47]

◆◆◆

CHARLES EDWARD CARRYL

THE WALLOPING WINDOW-BLIND

A capital ship for an ocean trip
　Was *The Walloping Window-
　blind*;
No gale that blew dismayed her crew
　Or troubled the captain's mind.
The man at the wheel was taught to
　feel
Contempt for the wildest blow,
And it often appeared, when the
　weather had cleared,
That he'd been in his bunk below.

The boatswain's mate was very
　sedate,
Yet fond of amusement, too;
And he played hopscotch with the
　starboard watch
While the captain tickled the
　crew.
And the gunner we had was appar-
　ently mad,
For he sat on the after-rail,
And fired salutes with the captain's
　boots,
In the teeth of the booming gale.

The captain sat in a commodore's
　hat,
And dined, in a royal way,
On toasted pigs and pickles and figs
And gummery bread, each day.
But the cook was Dutch, and be-
　haved as such;
For the food that he gave the crew
Was a number of tons of hot-cross
　buns,
Chopped up with sugar and glue.

And we all felt ill as mariners will,
　On a diet that's cheap and rude;
And we shivered and shook as we
　dipped the cook
In a tub of his gluesome food.
Then nautical pride we laid aside,
And we cast the vessel ashore
On the Gulliby Isles, where the
　Poohpooh smiles,
And the Anagazanders roar.

Composed of sand was that favored
　land,
And trimmed with cinnamon
　straws;
And pink and blue was the pleasing
　hue
Of the Tickletoeteaser's claws.
And we sat on the edge of a sandy
　ledge
And shot at the whistling bee;
And the Binnacle-bats wore water-
　proof hats
As they danced in the sounding
　sea.

On rubagub bark, from dawn to dark,
　We fed, till we all had grown
Uncommonly shrunk,—when a
　Chinese junk
Came by from the torriby zone.
She was stubby and square, but we
　didn't much care,
And we cheerily put to sea;
And we left the crew of the junk to
　chew
The bark of the rubagub tree.

THE HIGHLANDER'S SONG

There was a little pickle and he
　hadn't any name—
In this respect, I'm just informed,
　all pickles are the same.

[48]

A large policeman came along, a-swinging of his club,
And took that little pickle up and put him in a tub.

ROBINSON CRUSOE'S STORY

The night was thick and hazy
When the *Piccadilly Daisy*
Carried down the crew and captain in the sea;
And I think the water drowned 'em,
For they never, never found 'em,
And I know they didn't come ashore with me.

Oh! 'twas very sad and lonely
When I found myself the only
Population on this cultivated shore;
But I've made a little tavern
In a rocky little cavern,
And I sit and watch for people at the door.

I spent no time in looking
For a girl to do my cooking,
As I'm quite a clever hand at making stews;
But I had that fellow Friday
Just to keep the tavern tidy,
And to put a Sunday polish on my shoes.

I have a little garden
That I'm cultivating lard in,
As the things I eat are rather tough and dry;
For I live on toasted lizards,
Prickly pears and parrot gizzards,
And I'm really very fond of beetle pie.

The clothes I had were furry,
And it made me fret and worry
When I found the moths were eating off the hair;
And I had to scrape and sand 'em,
And I boiled 'em and I tanned 'em,
Till I got the fine morocco suit I wear.

I sometimes seek diversion
In a family excursion,
With the few domestic animals you see;
And we take along a carrot
As refreshment for the parrot,
And a little can of jungleberry tea.

Then we gather, as we travel,
Bits of moss and dirty gravel,
And we chip off little specimens of stone;
And we carry home as prizes
Funny bugs, of handy sizes,
Just to give the day a scientific tone.

If the roads are wet and muddy
We remain at home and study,—
For the Goat is very clever at a sum,—
And the Dog, instead of fighting,
Studies ornamental writing,
While the Cat is taking lessons on the drum.

We retire at eleven,
And we rise again at seven;
And I wish to call attention, as I close,
To the fact that all the scholars
Are correct about their collars,
And particular in turning out their toes.

THE POST CAPTAIN

When they heard the Captain humming and beheld the dancing crew,

[49]

On the *Royal Biddy* frigate was Sir
    Peter Bombazoo;
His mind was full of music and his
    head was full of tunes,
And he cheerfully exhibited on
    pleasant afternoons.

He could whistle, on his fingers, an
    invigorating reel,
And could imitate a piper on the
    handles of the wheel;
He could play in double octaves, too,
    all up and down the rail,
Or rattle off a rondo on the bottom
    of a pail.

Then porters with their packages
    and bakers with their buns,
And countesses in carriages and
    grenadiers with guns,
And admirals and commodores ar-
    rived from near and far,
To listen to the music of this enter-
    taining tar.

When they heard the captain hum-
    ming and beheld the dancing crew,
The commodores severely said,
    "Why, this will never do!"
And the admirals all hurried home,
    remarking, "This is most
Extraordinary conduct for a captain
    at his post."

Then they sent some sailing orders
    to Sir Peter, in a boat,
And he did a little fifing on the edges
    of the note;
But he read the sailing orders, as of
    course he had to do,
And removed the *Royal Biddy* to
    the Bay of Boohgabooh.

Now, Sir Peter took it kindly, but
    it's proper to explain

He was sent to catch a pirate out
    upon the Spanish Main.
And he played, with variations, an
    imaginary tune
On the buttons of his waistcoat, like
    a jocular bassoon.

Then a topman saw the pirate come
    a-sailing in the bay,
And reported to the captain in the
    ordinary way.
"I'll receive him," said Sir Peter,
    "with a musical salute,"
And he gave some imitations of a
    double-jointed flute.

Then the Pirate cried derisively,
    "I've heard it done before!"
And he hoisted up a banner em-
    blematical of gore.
But Sir Peter said serenely, "You
    may double-shot the guns
While I sing my little ballad of 'The
    Butter on the Buns.'"

Then the Pirate banged Sir Peter
    and Sir Peter banged him back,
And they banged away together as
    they took another tack.
Then Sir Peter said, politely, "You
    may board him, if you like,"
And he played a little dirge upon
    the handle of a pike.

Then the "Biddies" poured like hor-
    nets down upon the Pirate's deck
And Sir Peter caught the Pirate and
    he took him by the neck,
And remarked, "You must excuse
    me, but you acted like a brute
When I gave my imitation of that
    double-jointed flute."

So they took that wicked Pirate and
    they took his wicked crew,

And tied them up with double knots
  in packages of two.
And left them lying on their backs
  in rows upon the beach
With a little bread and water within
  comfortable reach.

Now the Pirate had a treasure
  (mostly silverware and gold),
And Sir Peter took and stowed it in
  the bottom of his hold;
And said, "I will retire on this cargo
  of doubloons,
And each of you, my gallant crew,
  may have some silver spoons."

Now commodores in coach-and-
  fours and corporals in cabs,
And men with carts of pies and tarts
  and fishermen with crabs,
And barristers with wigs, in gigs,
  still gather on the strand,
But there isn't any music save a little
  German band.

◇◇◇

GUY WETMORE CARRYL

THE FEARFUL FINALE OF THE IRASCIBLE MOUSE

Upon a stairway built of brick
  A pleasant-featured clock
From time to time would murmur
  "Tick"
And vary it with "Tock":
Although no great intelligence
  There lay in either word,
They were not meant to give offense
  To anyone who heard.

Within the pantry of the house,
  Among some piles of cheese,
There dwelt an irritable mouse,

Extremely hard to please:
His appetite was most immense.
  Each day he ate a wedge
Of Stilton cheese. In consequence
  His nerves were all on edge.

With ill-concealed impatience he,
  Upon his morning walk,
Had heard the clock unceasingly,
  Monotonously talk,
Until his rage burst every bound.
  He gave a fretful shout:
"Well, sakes alive! It's time I found
  What all this talk's about!"

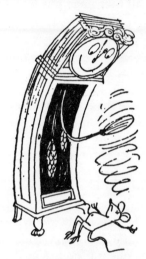

With all the admirable skill
  That marks the rodent race
The mouse ran up the clock, until
  He'd crept behind the face,
And then, with words that no one
  ought
To use, and scornful squeals
He cried aloud: "Just what I
  thought!
Great oaf, you're full of wheels!"

The timepiece sternly said, "Have
  done!"
And through the silent house

It struck emphatically one.
  (But that one was the mouse!)
To earth the prowling rodent fell,
  In terror for his life,
And turned to flee, but, sad to tell,
  There stood the farmer's wife.

She did not faint, she did not quail,
  She did not cry out: "Scat!"
She simply took him by the tail
And gave him to the cat,
And, with a stern, triumphant look,
  She watched him clawed and cleft,
And with some blotting paper took
  Up all that there was left.

THE MORAL: In a farmer's home
  Run down his herds, his flocks,
Run down his crops, run down his
    loam,
  But when it comes to clocks,
Pray leave them ticking every one
  In peace upon their shelves:
When running down is to be done
  The clocks run down themselves.

LITTLE RED RIDING HOOD

Most worthy of praise were the vir-
    tuous ways
  Of Little Red Riding Hood's ma,
And no one was ever more cautious
    and clever
  Than Little Red Riding Hood's
    pa.
They never misled, for they meant
    what they said,
  And frequently said what they
    meant.
They were careful to show her the
    way she should go,
  And the way that they showed her
    she went.
    For obedience she was effusively
    thanked,

And for anything else she was
  carefully spanked.

It thus isn't strange that Red Riding
    Hood's range
  Of virtues so steadily grew,
That soon she won prizes of various
    sizes,
  And golden encomiums too.
As a general rule she was head of
    her school,
  And at six was so notably smart
That they gave her a check for re-
    citing "The Wreck
  Of the Hesperus" wholly by heart.
And you all will applaud her
    the more, I am sure,
  When I add that the money
    she gave to the poor.

At eleven this lass had a Sunday-
    school class,
  At twelve wrote a volume of verse,
At fourteen was yearning for glory,
    and learning
  To be a professional nurse.
To a glorious height the young para-
    gon might
  Have climbed, if not nipped in
    the bud,
But the following year struck her
    smiling career
  With a dull and a sickening thud!
    (I have shed a great tear at the
    thought of her pain,
  And must copy my manuscript
    over again!)
Not dreaming of harm, one day on
    her arm
  A basket she hung. It was filled
With drinks made of spices, and
    jellies, and ices,
  And chicken wings, carefully
    grilled,

[52]

And a savory stew, and a novel or
  two
She persuaded a neighbor to loan,
And a Japanese fan, and a hot-water
  can,
  And a bottle of eau de cologne,
  And the rest of the things that
  your family fill
  Your room with whenever you
  chance to be ill.
She expected to find her decrepit
  but kind
Old grandmother waiting her call,
Exceedingly ill. Oh, that face on the
  pillow
  Did not look familiar at all!
With a whitening cheek she started
  to speak,
But her peril she instantly saw:
Her grandma had fled and she'd
  tackled instead
  Four merciless paws and a maw!
  When the neighbors came run-
  ning the wolf to subdue,
  He was licking his chops—and
  Red Riding Hood's, too!
At this terrible tale some readers
  will pale,
And others with horror grow
  dumb,
And yet it was better, I fear, he
  should get her—
  Just think what she might have
  become!
For an infant so keen might in future
  have been
A woman of awful renown,
Who carried on fights for her femi-
  nine rights,
  As the Mayor of an Arkansas
  town,
Or she might have continued the
  sins of her 'teens

And come to write verse for the Big
  Magazines!

THE MORAL: There's nothing much
  glummer
Than children whose talents
  appal.
One much prefers those that are
  dumber.
  And as for the paragons small—
If a swallow cannot make a summer,
  It can bring on a summary fall!

THE SYCOPHANTIC FOX AND
THE GULLIBLE RAVEN

A raven sat upon a tree,
  And not a word he spoke, for
His beak contained a piece of Brie,
  Or, maybe, it was Roquefort:
  We'll make it any kind you
  please—
  At all events, it was a cheese.

Beneath the tree's umbrageous limb
  A hungry fox sat smiling;
He saw the raven watching him,
  And spoke in words beguiling.
  "J'admire," said he, "ton beau
  plumage."
  (The which was simply persi-
  flage.)

Two things there are, no doubt you
  know,
  To which a fox is used:
A rooster that is bound to crow,
  A crow that's bound to roost,
  And whichsoever he espies
  He tells the most unblushing
  lies.

"Sweet fowl," he said, "I under-
  stand
  You're more than merely natty,
I hear you sing to beat the band
  And Adelina Patti.

[53]

Pray render with your liquid
tongue
A bit from 'Götterdäm-
merung.' "
This subtle speech was aimed to
please
The crow, and it succeeded:
He thought no bird in all the trees
Could sing as well as he did.
In flattery completely doused,
He gave the "Jewel Song" from
"Faust."
But gravitation's law, of course,
As Isaac Newton showed it,
Exerted on the cheese its force,
And elsewhere soon bestowed it.
In fact, there is no need to tell
What happened when to earth
it fell.
I blush to add that when the bird
Took in the situation
He said one brief, emphatic word,
Unfit for publication.
The fox was greatly startled,
but
He only sighed and answered
"Tut."
THE MORAL is: A fox is bound
To be a shameless sinner.
And also: When the cheese comes
round
You know it's after dinner.
But (what is only known to
few)
The fox is after dinner, too.

◇◇◇

G. K. CHESTERTON
A DEDICATION
(To E. C. B.)
He was, through boyhood's storm
and shower,

My best, my dearest friend;
We wore one hat, smoked one cigar
One standing at each end.

◇◇◇

ROBERT CLAIRMONT
THE ANSWERS
"When did the world begin and
how?"
I asked a lamb, a goat, a cow:
"What's it all about and why?"
I asked a hog as he went by:

"Where will the whole thing end
   and when?"
I asked a duck, a goose, a hen:

And I copied all the answers too,
A quack, a honk, an oink, a moo.

◇◇◇

E. E. CUMMINGS
IN JUST SPRING

in Just-
spring   when the world is mud-
luscious the little
lame balloonman

whistles   far   and wee

and eddieandbill come
running from marbles and
piracies and it's
spring

when the world is puddle-wonderful

the queer
old balloonman whistles
far   and   wee
and bettyandisbel come dancing

from hop-scotch and jump-rope and

it's
spring
and
      the

           goat-footed

balloonMan   whistles
far
and
wee

◇◇◇

WALTER DE LA MARE
BONES

Said Mr. Smith, "I really cannot
Tell you, Dr. Jones—

The most peculiar pain I'm in—
   I think it's in my *bones*."

Said Dr. Jones, "Oh, Mr. Smith,
   That's nothing. Without doubt
We have a simple cure for that;
   It is to take them out."

He laid forthwith poor Mr. Smith
   Close-clamped upon the table,
And, cold as stone, took out his bone
   As fast as he was able.

And Smith said, "Thank you, thank
   you, thank you,"
And wished him a Good-day;
And with his parcel 'neath his arm
   He slowly moved away.

◇◇◇

ELLEN DOUGLAS
DELAND

A BACHELOR OF MAINE

Hezekiah Bettle was a bachelor of
   Maine,
But one morning he departed by a
   very early train.
"For fuel is so costly," said the
   frugal Hezekiah,
"I am forced to find a dwelling
   where I need not pay for fire."

He took a beeline southward till to
   Mexico he came,
And found there a volcano with a
   most eccentric name,
And he built him there a cottage,
   did this Hezekiah Bettle,
He built it near the summit of
   Mount Popocatapetl.

Whenever he desired to cook a
   mutton chop

He'd hang it by a lengthy string
right over from the top,
From the top of the volcano he
would hang it by a string
And there, until 'twas nicely cooked,
he'd let his dinner swing.

To get his boiling water he would
lower down a kettle,
Right down into the crater of Mount
Popocatapetl;
From the ashes of the mountain he
would light his meerschaum pipe,
And he felt as truly happy as a jolly
little snipe.

But one evening, as it happened,
there came by a grizzly bear,
And he was much astonished to see
Hezekiah there;
So he tapped him on the shoulder,
this poor Hezekiah Bettle,
Who straightway did fall over into
Popocatapetl.

◇◈◇

T. S. ELIOT

THE NAMING OF CATS

The naming of cats is a difficult
matter,
It isn't just one of your holiday
games;
You may think at first I'm as mad
as a hatter
When I tell you, a cat must have
THREE DIFFERENT
NAMES.
First of all, there's the name that
the family use daily,
Such as Peter, Augustus, Alonzo
or James,

Such as Victor or Jonathan, George
or Bill Bailey—
All of them sensible everyday
names.
There are fancier names if you think
they sound sweeter,
Some for the gentlemen, some
for the dames:
Such as Plato, Admetus, Electra,
Demeter—
But all of them sensible everyday
names.
But I tell you, a cat needs a name
that's particular,
A name that's peculiar, and more
dignified,
Else how can he keep up his tail
perpendicular,
Or spread out his whiskers, or
cherish his pride?
Of names of this kind, I can give
you a quorum,
Such as Munkustrap, Quaxo, or
Coricopat,
Such as Bombalurina, or else Jelly-
lorum—
Names that never belong to more
than one cat.
But above and beyond there's still
one name left over,
And that is the name that you
never will guess;
The name that no human research
can discover—
But THE CAT HIMSELF
KNOWS, and will never
confess.
When you notice a cat in profound
meditation,
The reason, I tell you, is always
the same:
His mind is engaged in a rapt con-
templation

Of the thought, of the thought,
    of the thought of his name:
His ineffable effable
    Effanineffable
Deep and inscrutable singular name.

◇◇◇

ANTHONY EUWER

MY FACE

As a beauty I am not a star,
There are others more handsome,
    by far,
    But my face—I don't mind it
    For I am behind it.
It's the people in front get the jar!

◇◇◇

EUGENE FIELD

THE LITTLE PEACH

A little peach in the orchard grew,
A little peach of emerald hue;
Warmed by the sun and wet by the
    dew,
    It grew.

One day, passing that orchard
    through,
That little peach dawned on the
    view
Of Johnny Jones and his sister Sue,
    Them two.

Up at that peach a club they threw,

Down from the stem on which it
    grew
Fell that peach of emerald hue.
    Mon Dieu!

John took a bite and Sue took a
    chew,
And then the trouble began to brew,
Trouble the doctor couldn't subdue.
    Too true!

Under the turf where the daisies
    grew
They planted John and his sister
    Sue,
And their little souls to the angels
    flew,
    Boo hoo!

What of that peach of the emerald
    hue;
Warmed by the sun and wet by the
    dew?
Ah, well, its mission on earth is
    through.
    Adieu!

◇◇◇

SAMUEL FOOTE

THE GREAT PANJANDRUM

So she went into the garden
to cut a cabbage leaf
to make an apple pie;
and at the same time
a great she-bear, coming down the
    street,
pops its head into the shop.
What! no soap?
    So he died,
and she very imprudently married
    the Barber:
and there were present
the Picninnies,

[57]

and the Joblillies,
    And the Garyulies,
and the great Panjandrum himself,
with the little round button at top;
and they all fell to playing the game
    of catch-as-catch-can,
till the gunpowder ran out at the
    heels of their boots.

◇◇◇

SAM WALTER FOSS

THE PRAYER OF CYRUS BROWN

"The proper way for a man to pray,"
    Said Deacon Lemuel Keyes,
"And the only proper attitude
    Is down upon his knees."

"No, I should say the way to pray,"
    Said Rev. Doctor Wise,
"Is standing straight with out-
        stretched arms
    And rapt and upturned eyes."

"Oh, no; no, no," said Elder Slow,
    "Such posture is too proud:
A man should pray with eyes fast
        closed
    And head contritely bowed."

"It seems to me his hands should be
    Austerely clasped in front,
With both thumbs pointing toward
        the ground,"
    Said Rev. Doctor Blunt.

"Las' year I fell in Hodgkin's well
    Head first," said Cyrus Brown,
"With both my heels a-stickin' up,
    My head a-pinting down;

"An' I made a prayer right then an'
        there—
    Best prayer I ever said,
The prayingest prayer I ever prayed,
    A-standing on my head."

◇◇◇

MARY E. WILKINS FREEMAN

THE OSTRICH IS A SILLY BIRD

The ostrich is a silly bird,
    With scarcely any mind.

He often runs so very fast,
    He leaves himself behind.

And when he gets there, has to stand
    And hang about till night,
Without a blessed thing to do
    Until he comes in sight.

◇◇◇

NORMAN GALE

BOBBY'S FIRST POEM

Itt rely is ridikkelus
how uncle Charley tikkles us

[58]

at eester and at mikklemus
upon the nursry floor.

and rubbs our chins and bites our
  ears
like firty-fousand poler bares
and roars like lyons down the stares
and won't play enny more.

◇◇◇

W. S. GILBERT

THE POLICEMAN'S LOT

When a felon's not engaged in his
  employment,
  Or maturing his felonious little
    plans,
His capacity for innocent enjoyment
  Is just as great as any other man's.
Our feelings we with difficulty
  smother
  When constabulary duty's to be
    done:
Ah, take one consideration with
  another,
  A policeman's lot is not a happy
    one.
When the enterprising burglar's not
  a-burgling,

And the cutthroat isn't occupied
  in crime,
He loves to hear the little brook a-
  gurgling,
  And listen to the merry village
    chime.
When the coster's finished jumping
  on his mother,
  He loves to lie a-basking in the
    sun:
Ah, take one consideration with
  another,
  A policeman's lot is not a happy
    one!

THE YARN OF THE NANCY BELL

'Twas on the shores that round our
  coast
  From Deal to Ramsgate span,
That I found alone on a piece of
  stone
  An elderly naval man.

His hair was weedy, his beard was
  long,
  And weedy and long was he,

And I heard this wight on the shore
    recite,
  In a singular minor key:

"Oh, I am a cook and a captain
    bold,
  And the mate of the *Nancy* brig,
And a bo'sun tight, and a midship-
    mite,
  And the crew of the captain's
    gig."

And he shook his fists and he tore
    his hair,
  Till I really felt afraid,
For I couldn't help thinking the
    man had been drinking,
  And so I simply said:

"Oh, elderly man, it's little I know
  Of the duties of men of the sea,
And I'll eat my hand if I understand
  How you can possibly be

"At once a cook, and a captain bold,
  And the mate of the *Nancy* brig,
And a bo'sun tight, and a midship-
    mite,
  And the crew of the captain's
    gig."

Then he gave a hitch to his trousers,
    which
  Is a trick all seamen larn,
And having got rid of a thumping
    quid,
  He spun this painful yarn:

" 'Twas in the good ship *Nancy Bell*
  That we sailed to the Indian Sea,
And there on a reef we come to grief,
  Which has often occurred to me.

"And pretty nigh all the crew was
    drowned
  (There was seventy-seven o' soul),

And only ten of the *Nancy's* men
  Said 'Here!' to the muster roll.

"There was me and the cook and
    the captain bold,
  And the mate of the *Nancy* brig,
And the bo'sun tight, and a mid-
    shipmite,
  And the crew of the captain's gig.

"For a month we'd neither wittles
    nor drink,
  Till a-hungry we did feel,
So we drawed a lot, and accordin'
    shot
  The captain for our meal.

"The next lot fell to the *Nancy's*
    mate,
  And a delicate dish he made;
Then our appetite with the mid-
    shipmite
  We seven survivors stayed.

"And then we murdered the bos'un
    tight,
  And he much resembled pig;
Then we wittled free, did the cook
    and me,
  On the crew of the captain's gig.

"Then only the cook and me was
    left,
  And the delicate question, 'Which
Of us two goes to the kettle?' arose,
  And we argued it out as sich.

"For I loved that cook as a brother,
    I did,
  And the cook he worshipped me;
But we'd both be blowed if we'd
    either be stowed
  In the other chap's hold, you see.

" 'I'll be eat if you dines off me,'
    says Tom.

'Yes, that,' says I, 'you'll be,—
I'm boiled if I die, my friend,'
    quoth I.
And 'Exactly so,' quoth he.

"Says he, 'Dear James, to murder
    me
Were a foolish thing to do,
For don't you see that you can't
    cook *me*,
    While I can—and will—cook
    you!'

"So he boils the water, and takes
    the salt
And the pepper in portions true
(Which he never forgot), and some
    chopped shalot,
And some sage and parsley too.

" 'Come here,' says he, with a proper
    pride,
Which his smiling features tell,
' 'Twill soothing be if I let you see
How extremely nice you'll smell.'

"And he stirred it round and round
    and round,
And he sniffed at the foaming
    froth;
When I ups with his heels, and
    smothers his squeals
In the scum of the boiling broth.

"And I eat that cook in a week or
    less,
And—as I eating be
The last of his chops, why, I almost
    drops,
For a wessel in sight I see.

"And I never grin, and I never smile,
And I never larf or play,
But sit and croak, and a single joke
I have—which is to say:

"Oh, I am a cook and a captain bold,
    And the mate of the *Nancy* brig,
And a bos'un tight, and a midship-
    mite,
    And the crew of the captain's
    gig!"

From THE LORD
CHANCELLOR'S SONG

When you're lying awake with a
    dismal headache, and repose is
    tabooed by anxiety,
I conceive you may use any lan-
    guage you choose to indulge in,
    without impropriety;
For your brain is on fire—the bed-
    clothes conspire of usual slumber
    to plunder you:
First your counterpane goes and
    uncovers your toes, and your sheet
    slips demurely from under you;
Then the blanketing tickles—you
    feel like mixed pickles—so terribly
    sharp is the pricking,
And you're hot, and you're cross,
    and you tumble and toss till
    there's nothing 'twixt you and
    the ticking.
Then the bedclothes all creep to
    the ground in a heap, and you
    pick 'em all up in a tangle;
Next your pillow resigns and politely
    declines to remain at its usual
    angle!
Well, you get some repose in the
    form of a doze, with hot eyeballs
    and head ever aching,
But your slumbering teems with
    such horrible dreams that you'd
    very much better be waking;
For you dream you are crossing the
    Channel, and tossing about in a
    steamer from Harwich—

Which is something between a large
bathing machine and a very small
second-class carriage—

* * *

You're a regular wreck, with a crick
in your neck, and no wonder you
snore, for your head's on the
floor, and you've needles and pins
from your soles to your shins, and
your flesh is a-creep, for your left
leg's asleep, and you've cramp in
your toes, and a fly on your nose,
and some fluff in your lung, and a
feverish tongue, and a thirst that's
intense, and a general sense that
you haven't been sleeping in
clover;
But the darkness has passed, and it's
daylight at last, and the night has
been long—ditto ditto my song—
and thank goodness they're both
of them over!

CAPTAIN REECE

Of all the ships upon the blue
No ship contained a better crew
Than that of worthy Captain Reece,
Commander of *The Mantelpiece*.

He was adored by all his men,
For worthy Captain Reece, R.N.,
Did all that lay within him to
Promote the comfort of his crew.

If ever they were dull or sad,
Their captain danced to them like
mad,
Or told, to make the time pass by,
Droll legends of his infancy.

A feather bed had every man,
Warm slippers and hot-water can,

Brown windsor from the captain's
store,
A valet, too, to every four.

Did they with thirst in summer
burn?
Lo, seltzogenes at every turn,
And on all very sultry days
Cream ices handed round on trays.

Then currant wine and ginger pops
Stood handily on all the "tops";
And, also, with amusement rife,
A "Zoetrope, or Wheel of Life."

New volumes came across the sea
From Mister Mudie's libraree;
The Times and *Saturday Review*
Beguiled the leisure of the crew.

Kindhearted Captain Reece, R. N.,
Was quite devoted to his men;
In point of fact, good Captain Reece
Beatified *The Mantelpiece*.

One summer eve, at half past ten,
He said (addressing all his men),
"Come, tell me, please, what I can
do,
To please and gratify my crew.

"By any reasonable plan
I'll make you happy if I can;
My own convenience count as *nil*;
It is my duty, and I will."

Then up and answered William Lee
(The kindly captain's coxswain he,
A nervous, shy, low-spoken man);
He cleared his throat and thus
began:

"You have a daughter, Captain
Reece,
Ten female cousins and a niece,
A ma, if what I'm told is true,
Six sisters, and an aunt or two.

"Now, somehow, sir, it seems to
    me,
More friendly-like we all should be,
If you united of 'em to
Unmarried members of the crew.

"If you'd ameliorate our life,
Let each select from them a wife;
And as for nervous me, old pal,
Give me your own enchanting gal!"

Good Captain Reece, that worthy
    man,
Debated on his coxswain's plan:
"I quite agree," he said, "O Bill;
It is my duty, and I will.

"My daughter, that enchanting girl,
Has just been promised to an earl,
And all my other familee,
To peers of various degree.

"But what are dukes and viscounts
    to
The happiness of all my crew?
The word I gave you I'll fulfill;
It is my duty, and I will.

"As you desire it shall befall,
I'll settle thousands on you all.
And I shall be, despite my hoard,
The only bachelor on board."

The boatswain of *The Mantelpiece*,
He blushed and spoke to Captain
    Reece.
"I beg your honor's leave," he said,
"If you would wish to go and wed,

"I have a widowed mother who
Would be the very thing for you—
She long has loved you from afar,
She washes for you, Captain R."

The captain saw the dame that
    day—
Addressed her in his playful way—

"And did it want a wedding ring?
It was a tempting ickle sing!

"Well, well, the chaplain I will
    seek,
We'll all be married this day week
At yonder church upon the hill;
It is my duty, and I will!"

The sisters, cousins, aunts, and
    niece,
And widowed ma of Captain Reece,
Attended there as they were bid;
It was their duty, and they did.

THE DUKE OF PLAZA-TORO

In enterprise of martial kind,
    When there was any fighting,
He led his regiment from behind
    (He found it less exciting).
But when away his regiment ran,
    His place was at the fore, O—
        That celebrated,
        Cultivated,
        Underrated
            Nobleman,
    The Duke of Plaza-Toro!
In the first and foremost flight, ha,
    ha!
You always found that knight, ha,
    ha!
        That celebrated,
        Cultivated,
        Underrated
            Nobleman,
    The Duke of Plaza-Toro!

When, to evade Destruction's hand,
    To hide they all proceeded,
No soldier in that gallant band
    Hid half as well as he did.
He lay concealed throughout the
    war,
    And so preserved his gore, O!

[63]

That unaffected,
Undetected,
Well connected
Warrior,
The Duke of Plaza-Toro!
In every doughty deed, ha, ha!
He always took the lead, ha, ha!
That unaffected,
Undetected,
Well connected
Warrior,
The Duke of Plaza-Toro!

When told that they would all be
   shot
Unless they left the service,
That hero hesitated not,
So marvellous his nerve is.
He sent his resignation in,
   The first of all his corps, O!
That very knowing,
Overflowing,
Easygoing
Paladin,
The Duke of Plaza-Toro!
To men of grosser clay, ha, ha!
He always showed the way, ha, ha!
That very knowing,
Overflowing,
Easygoing
Paladin,
The Duke of Plaza-Toro!

ETIQUETTE

The *Ballyshannon* foundered off
   the coast of Cariboo,
And down in fathoms many went
   the captain and the crew;
Down went the owners—greedy men
   whom hope of gain allured:
Oh, dry the starting tear, for they
   were heavily insured.

Besides the captain and the mate,
   the owners and the crew,
The passengers were also drowned
   excepting only two:
Young Peter Gray, who tasted teas
   for Baker, Croop, and Co.,
And Somers, who from Eastern
   shores imported indigo.

These passengers, by reason of their
   clinging to a mast,
Upon a desert island were eventu-
   ally cast.
They hunted for their meals, as
   Alexander Selkirk used,
But they couldn't chat together—
   they had not been introduced.

For Peter Gray, and Somers, too,
   though certainly in trade,
Were properly particular about the
   friends they made;
And somehow thus they settled it,
   without a word of mouth,
That Gray should take the northern
   half, while Somers took the south.

On Peter's portion oysters grew—
   a delicacy rare,
But oysters were a delicacy Peter
   couldn't bear.
On Somer's side was turtle, on the
   shingle lying thick,
Which Somers couldn't eat, because it always made him sick.

Gray gnashed his teeth with envy
   as he saw a mighty store
Of turtle unmolested on his fellow
   creature's shore.
The oysters at his feet aside im-
   patiently he shoved,
For turtle and his mother were the
   only things he loved.

And Somers sighed in sorrow as he
 settled in the south,
For the thought of Peter's oysters
 brought the water to his mouth.
He longed to lay him down upon
 the shelly bed, and stuff:
He had often eaten oysters, but had
 never had enough.

How they wished an introduction to
 each other they had had
When on board the *Ballyshannon!*
 And it drove them nearly mad
To think how very friendly with
 each other they might get,
If it wasn't for the arbitrary rule of
 etiquette!

One day, when out a-hunting for
 the *mus ridiculus,*
Gray overheard his fellow man solil-
 oquising thus:
"I wonder how the playmates of
 my youth are getting on,
M'Connell, S. B. Walters, Paddy
 Byles, and Robinson?"

These simple words made Peter as
 delighted as could be;
Old chummies at the Charterhouse
 were Robinson and he.
He walked straight up to Somers,
 then he turned extremely red,
Hesitated, hummed and hawed a
 bit, then cleared his throat, and
 said:

"I beg your pardon—pray forgive
 me if I seem too bold,
But you have breathed a name I
 knew familiarly of old.
You spoke aloud of Robinson—I
 happened to be by.
You know him?" "Yes, extremely
 well." "Allow me, so do I."

It was enough: they felt they could
 more pleasantly get on,
For (ah, the magic of the fact!)
 they each knew Robinson!
And Mr. Somers' turtle was at
 Peter's service quite,
And Mr. Somers punished Peter's
 oyster beds all night.

They soon became like brothers
 from community of wrongs;
They wrote each other little odes
 and sang each other songs;
They told each other anecdotes dis-
 paraging their wives;
On several occasions, too, they saved
 each other's lives.

They felt quite melancholy when
 they parted for the night,
And got up in the morning soon
 as ever it was light;
Each other's pleasant company they
 reckoned so upon,
And all because it happened that
 they both knew Robinson!

They lived for many years on that
 inhospitable shore,
And day by day they learned to love
 each other more and more.
At last, to their astonishment, on
 getting up one day,
They saw a frigate anchored in the
 offing of the bay.

To Peter an idea occurred. "Suppose
 we cross the main?
So good an opportunity may not be
 found again."
And Somers thought a minute, then
 ejaculated, "Done!
I wonder how my business in the
 City's getting on?"

"But stay," said Mr. Peter; "when
in England, as you know,
I earned a living tasting teas for
Baker, Croop, and Co.,
I may be superseded—my employers
think me dead!"
"Then come with me," said Somers,
"and taste indigo instead."

But all their plans were scattered in
a moment when they found
The vessel was a convict ship from
Portland outward bound;
When a boat came off to fetch them,
though they felt it very kind,
To go on board they firmly but re-
spectfully declined.

As both the happy settlers roared
with laughter at the joke,
They recognized a gentlemanly fellow pulling stroke:
'Twas Robinson—a convict, in an
unbecoming frock!
Condemned to seven years for mis-
appropriating stock!!!

They laughed no more, for Somers
thought he had been rather rash
In knowing one whose friend had
misappropriated cash;
And Peter thought a foolish tack
he must have gone upon
In making the acquaintance of a
friend of Robinson.

At first they didn't quarrel very
openly, I've heard;
They nodded when they met, and
now and then exchanged a word:
The word grew rare, and rarer still
the nodding of the head.
And when they meet each other
now, they cut each other dead.

To allocate the island they agreed
by word of mouth,
And Peter takes the north again, and
Somers takes the south;
And Peter has the oysters, which
he hates, in layers thick,
And Somers has the turtle—turtle
always makes him sick.

GENERAL JOHN

The bravest names for fire and
flames
And all that mortal durst,
Were GENERAL JOHN and PRIVATE
JAMES,
Of the Sixty-seventy-first.

GENERAL JOHN was a soldier tried,
A chief of warlike dons;
A haughty stride and a withering
pride
Were MAJOR-GENERAL JOHN'S.

A sneer would play on his martial
phiz,
Superior birth to show;
"Pish!" was a favorite word of his,
And he often said "Ho! ho!"

FULL-PRIVATE JAMES described
might be,
As a man of a mournful mind;
No characteristic trait had he
Of any distinctive kind.

From the ranks, one day, cried
PRIVATE JAMES,
"Oh! MAJOR-GENERAL JOHN,
I've doubts of our respective names,
My mournful mind upon.

"A glimmering thought occurs to
me
(Its source I can't unearth),

[66]

But I've a kind of a notion we
    Were cruelly changed at birth.

"I've a strange idea that each other's
    names
We've each of us here got on.
Such things have been," said PRI-
    VATE JAMES.
    "They have!" sneered GENERAL
    JOHN.

"My GENERAL JOHN, I swear upon
    My oath I think 'tis so——"
"Pish!" proudly sneered his GEN-
    ERAL JOHN,
    And he also said "Ho! ho!"

"My GENERAL JOHN! my GENERAL
    JOHN!
My GENERAL JOHN!" quoth he,
"This aristocratical sneer upon
    Your face I blush to see!

"No truly great or generous cove
    Deserving of them names,
Would sneer at a fixed idea that's
    drove
    In the mind of a PRIVATE JAMES!"

Said GENERAL JOHN, "Upon your
    claims
No need your breath to waste;
If this is a joke, FULL-PRIVATE
    JAMES,
    It's a joke of doubtful taste.

"But, being a man of doubtless
    worth,
    If you feel certain quite
That we were probably changed at
    birth,
    I'll venture to say you're right."

So GENERAL JOHN as PRIVATE JAMES
    Fell in, parade upon;

And PRIVATE JAMES, by change of
    names,
    Was MAJOR-GENERAL JOHN.

THERE WAS A YOUNG MAN OF ST. BEES

There was a young man of St. Bees
Who was stung on the arm by a
    wasp.
    When they asked, "Does it hurt?"
    He replied, "No, it doesn't,
But I thought all the time 'twas a
    hornet."

❖❖❖

HARRY GRAHAM

COMMON SENSE

"There's been an accident!" they
    said,
"Your servant's cut in half; he's
    dead!"
"Indeed!" said Mr. Jones, "and
    please
Send me the half that's got my keys."

PATIENCE

When ski-ing in the Engadine
My hat blew off down a ravine.
My son, who went to fetch it back,
Slipped through an icy glacier's
    crack,
And then got permanently stuck.
It really was infernal luck;
My hat was practically new—
I loved my little Henry too—
And I may have to wait for years
Till either of them reappears.

TRAGEDY

Making toast by the fireside,
    Nurse fell in the fire and died;

And, to make it ten times worse,
All the toast was burned with
nurse.

PRESENCE OF MIND

When, with my little daughter
Blanche,
I climbed the Alps, last summer,
I saw a dreadful avalanche
About to overcome her;

And, as it swept her down the slope,
I vaguely wondered whether
I should be wise to cut the rope
That held us twain together.

I must confess I'm glad I did,
But still I miss the child—poor kid!

QUIET FUN

My son Augustus, in the street, one
day,
Was feeling quite exceptionally
merry.
A stranger asked him: "Can you
show me, pray,
The quickest way to Brompton
Cemetery?"
"The quickest way? You bet I can!"
says Gus,
And pushed the fellow under-
neath a bus.

Whatever people say about my son,
He does enjoy his little bit of fun.

❖❖❖

KENNETH GRAHAME

THE SONG OF MR. TOAD

The world has held great Heroes,
As history-books have showed;

But never a name to go down to
fame
Compared with that of Toad!

The clever men at Oxford
Know all that there is to be
knowed.
But they none of them knew one
half as much
As intelligent Mr. Toad!

The animals sat in the Ark and
cried,
Their tears in torrents flowed.
Who was it said, "There's land
ahead"?
Encouraging Mr. Toad!

The Army all saluted
As they marched along the road.
Was it the King? Or Kitchener?
No. It was Mr. Toad!

The Queen and her Ladies-in-
waiting
Sat at the window and sewed.
She cried, "Look! who's that *hand-
some* man?"
They answered, "Mr. Toad."

❖❖❖

ARTHUR GUITERMAN

THE LEGEND OF THE FIRST
CAM-U-EL

Across the sands of Syria,
Or, possibly, Algeria,
Or some benighted neighborhood
of barrenness and
drouth,
There came the Prophet
Sam-u-el
Upon the Only Cam-u-el—
A bumpy, grumpy quadruped of dis-
contented mouth.

The atmosphere was gluti-
nous;
The Cam-u-el was muti-
nous;
He dumped the pack from off his
back; with horrid grunts
and squeals
He made the desert hide-
ous;
With strategy perfidious
He tied his neck in curlicues, he
kicked his paddy heels.

Then quoth the gentle
Sam-u-el,
"You rogue. I ought to lam
you well!
Though zealously I've shielded you
from every grief and woe,
It seems, to voice a plati-
tude,
You haven't any gratitude.
I'd like to hear what cause you have
for doing thus and so!"

To him replied the Cam-
u-el,
"I beg your pardon, Sam-
u-el.
I know that I'm a Reprobate, I know
that I'm a Freak;
But, oh! this utter loneli-
ness!
My too-distinguished Onli-
ness!
Were there but other Cam-u-els I
wouldn't be unique."

The Prophet beamed be-
guilingly.
"Aha," he answered, smil-
ingly,
"You feel the need of company? I
clearly understand.

We'll speedily create for
you
The corresponding mate
for you—
Ho! presto, change-o, dinglebat!"—
he waved a potent hand,

And, lo! from out vacuity
A second Incongruity,
To wit, a lady Cam-u-el was born
through magic art.
Her structure anatomical,
Her form and face were
comical;
She was, in short, a Cam-u-el, the
other's counterpart.

As Spaniards gaze on Ara-
gon,
Upon that female paragon
So gazed the Prophet's Cam-u-el,
that primal desert ship.
A connoisseur meticulous,
He found her that ridicu-
lous
He grinned from ear to auricle *until
he split his lip!*

Because of his temerity
That Cam-u-el's posterity
Must wear divided upper lips
through all their solemn
lives!
A prodigy astonishing
Reproachfully admonish-
ing
Those wicked, heartless married
men who ridicule their
wives.

QWERTY-Ù-I-OP

My typewriter, I gather
from her lettered row on top,
Should answer to the comely name
of

"Qwerty-ù-i-op."
She clicks away as gaily as the cricket
in the dell,
And at the proper moment tintin-
nabulates a bell.

She hammers out the symbols and
arranges them in line;
And though her spelling's perfect
and her punctuation's fine,
She gets no monthly wages for her
unremitting toil
Except a new black ribbon and a
drop or two of oil.

She dots her *i's* correctly and she
crosses all her *t's*;
She never drops her *h's* and she always writes with *e's*;
She never interrupts me to intrude
her private views,
But earns me *V's* and *X's* while she
minds her *p's* and *q's*.

I've never had a working-mate in
studio or shop
More faithful and dependable than
Qwertyuiop;
She asks no foolish questions and
she never does amiss;
I feed her sheets of paper and she
rhymes me things like this.

ROUTINE

No matter what we are and who,
Some duties everyone must do:

A Poet puts aside his wreath
To wash his face and brush his teeth,

And even Earls
Must comb their curls,

And even Kings
Have underthings.

IN PRAISE OF LLAMAS

La-la-llamas rate as mammals
Much resembling baby camels,
And their appellation's hard to speak
and spell,
For it seems, when Adam ut-
tered
Their baptismal name, he stut-
tered,
Hence we always must reduplicate
the "L."

Those Peruvians, the Incas,
On their lonely mountain fincas
(Which is Spanish for plantations,
ranches, farms)
Reared, instead of Leghorns,
Brahmas
And Minorcas, La-la-llamas
With Alpacas who have correspond-
ing charms.

Through Andean panoramas
Wind the herds of La-la-llamas,
Skirting precipices dangerously
steep,
Over swinging bridge or ferry
To some La-la-llamaserai,

Or wherever La-la-llamas stop to
  sleep.

Lively lambkin La-la-llamas
Trot beside their ma-ma-ma-
  mas,
Lightly dancing when their parents
  pause to graze;
Lovely lady La-la-llamas
Look like queens of movie dra-
  mas
With their melting eyes and soft,
  coquettish ways.

And they splash across lagunas
With their cousins, the Vicunas
And Guanacos, bearing loads upon
  their backs;
And these useful La-la-llamas
Furnish wool to make pajamas
And to help their owners pay the
  income tax.

So be happy, La-la-llamas
Climbing Western Fujiyamas
Or descending to the vega's fertile
  floor!
Thrive and flourish, La-la-lla-
  mas,
In a clime like Alabama's,
In Boliva, Peru and Ecuador!

HABITS OF THE HIPPOPOTAMUS

The hippopotamus is strong
And huge of head and broad of
  bustle;
The limbs on which he rolls along
Are big with hippopotomuscle.

He does not greatly care for sweets
Like ice cream, apple pie, or cus-
  tard,
But takes to flavor what he eats
A little hippopotomustard.

The hippopotamus is true
To all his principles, and just;
He always tries his best to do
The things one hippopotomust

He never rides in trucks or trams
In taxicabs or omnibuses,
And so keeps out of traffic jams
And other hippopotomusses.

❖❖❖

BRET HARTE

PLAIN LANGUAGE FROM TRUTHFUL JAMES

Which I wish to remark,
And my language is plain,
That for ways that are dark
And for tricks that are vain,
The heathen Chinee is peculiar,
Which the same I would rise to
  explain.

Ah Sin was his name;
And I shall not deny,
In regard to the same,
What that name might imply;

But his smile it was pensive and
    childlike,
As I frequent remarked to Bill
    Nye.

It was August the third,
    And quite soft was the skies;
Which it might be inferred
    That Ah Sin was likewise;
Yet he played it that day upon
    William
And me in a way I despise.

Which we had a small game,
    And Ah Sin took a hand:
It was euchre. The same
    He did not understand;
But he smiled as he sat by the table,
    With the smile that was child-
    like and bland.

Yet the cards they were stocked
    In a way that I grieve,
And my feelings were shocked
    At the state of Nye's sleeve,
Which was stuffed full of aces and
    bowers,
    And the same with intent to de-
    ceive.

But the hands that were played
    By that heathen Chinee,
And the points that he made,
    Were quite frightful to see;
Till at last he put down a right
    bower,
    Which the same Nye had dealt
    unto me.

Then I looked up at Nye,
    And he gazed upon me;
And he rose with a sigh,
    And said, "Can this be?
We are ruined by Chinese cheap
    labor,"

And he went for that heathen
    Chinee.

In the scene that ensued
    I did not take a hand;
But the floor it was strewed
    Like the leaves on the strand,
With the cards that Ah Sin had
    been hiding,
    In the game "he did not under-
    stand."

In his sleeves, which were long,
    He had twenty-four jacks,
Which was coming it strong,
    Yet I state but the facts;
And we found on his nails, which
    were taper,
    What is frequent in tapers—that's
    wax.

Which is why I remark,
    And my language is plain,
That for ways that are dark
    And for tricks that are vain,
The heathen Chinee is peculiar,
    Which the same I am free to
    maintain.

◇◇◇

SIR A. P. HERBERT

SAVE THE TIGER!

When Lady Jane refused to be
The wife of Viscount Fiddledee
He rose abruptly from his knee
    And said, "Excuse this bungle—
I think I will not stay to dine,
There is a train at half-past-nine;
Tomorrow by the fastest line
    I'm leaving for the jungle.

"Ho, varlet, run and pack my gun,
My passport pray discover;

I mean to shoot some savage brute
  To show how much I love her.
Far off in India's poisoned swamps
Some unsuspecting tiger romps,
  Condemned to die;
  And you know why—
'Cos you won't marry me.
Oh, ain't you got no heart, my gal?
Think of that dumb animal.
    Save that tiger,
    Poor dumb tiger,
  Save that tiger—marry me!

"I'll hunt him down on shiny nights
With cunning telescopic sights,
And if the creature turns and bites,
  As is his cruel fashion,
I'll lie content and let him chew,
A-thinking all the time of you;
For what's the worst that he can do
  Compared with hopeless passion?

  "Ho, varlet, run and pack my gun,
  My lovely one rejects me.
I kind of ache to shoot a snake,
  For that's how it affects me.
With battle-ax and blunderbuss
I'll kill the hippopotamus;
    Some buffalo
    Has got to go
Because you won't be mine.
Heartless one, I'm better dead,
But think of that dumb quadruped;
    Save that python,
    Save that hippo,
  Save that Buffalo—be mine!"

The Lady Jane began to cry;
The thought of hippopotami
Unnaturally doomed to die
  Had stirred the woman's pity.
She married him. And till this day,
Whenever he would have his way,
He only had to sing or say
  This moving little ditty:

"Ho, pack my gun, you naughty
    one!
Although I love you madly,
I'm off to shoot some savage brute,
  You do behave so badly.
I'd like to beat you, but you'd laugh,
I'll take it out of some giraffe,
    Some buffalo
    Has got to go
Because you won't be good.
Ain't you got no heart, dear wife?
You can't approve of taking life—
    Then save that tiger,
    Poor dumb tiger,
  Save that buffalo—be good!"

❖❖❖

OLIVER HERFORD

STAIRS

Here's to the man who invented
    stairs
And taught our feet to soar!
He was the first who ever burst
Into a second floor.

The world would be downstairs to-
    day
Had he not found the key;
So let his name go down to fame,
Whatever it may be.

THE CROCODILE

Crocodile once dropped a line
To a Fox to invite him to dine;
  But the Fox wrote to say
  He was dining that day,
With a Bird friend, and begged to
  decline.

She sent off at once to a Goat.
"Pray don't disappoint me," she
    wrote;

But he answered too late,
He'd forgotten the date,
Having thoughtlessly eaten her note.

The Crocodile thought him ill-bred,
And invited two Rabbits instead;
But the Rabbits replied,
They were hopelessly tied
By a previous engagement, and fled.

Then she wrote in despair to some
    Eels,
And begged them to "drop in" to
    meals;
But the Eels left their cards
With their coldest regards,
And took to what went for their
    heels.

Cried the Crocodile then in disgust,
"My motives they seem to mistrust,
Their suspicions are base
Since they don't know their
    place,—
I suppose if I *must* starve, I *must!*"

JAPANESQUE

Oh, where the white quince blossom
    swings
I love to take my Japan ease!
I love the maid Anise who clings
So lightly on my Japan knees;

I love the little song she sings,
The little love-song Japanese.
I *almost* love the lute's *tink tunkle*
Played by that charming Jap
    Anise—
For am I not her old Jap uncle?
And is she not my Japan niece?

THE UNFORTUNATE GIRAFFE

There was once a giraffe who said,
    "What
Do I want with my tea strong or hot?
For my throat's such a length
The tea loses its strength,
And is cold ere it reaches the spot."

THE ARTFUL ANT

Once on a time an artful Ant
Resolved to give a ball,

For tho' in stature she was scant,
　She was not what you'd call
A shy or bashful little Ant.
　(She was not shy at all.)

She sent her invitations through
　The forest far and wide,
To all the Birds and Beasts she
　knew,
　And many more beside.
("You never know what you can
　do,"
Said she, "until you've tried.")

Five-score acceptances came in
　Faster than she could read.
Said she: "Dear me! I'd best begin
　To stir myself indeed!"
(A pretty pickle she was in,
　With five-score guests to feed!)

The artful Ant sat up all night,
　A-thinking o'er and o'er,
How she could make from nothing,
　quite
Enough to feed five-score.
(Between ourselves I think she
　might
Have thought of that before.)

She thought, and thought, and
　thought all night,
　And all the following day,
Till suddenly she struck a bright
　Idea, which was—(but stay!
Just what it was I am not quite
　At liberty to say).

Enough, that when the festal day
　Came round, the Ant was seen
To smile in a peculiar way,
　As if—(but you may glean
From seeing tragic actors play
　The kind of smile I mean).

From here and there and everywhere
　The happy creatures came,
The Fish alone could not be there.
　(And they were not to blame.
"They really could not stand the
　air,
　But thanked her just the same.")

They danced, and danced, and
　danced, and danced;
　It was a jolly sight!
They pranced, and pranced, and
　pranced, and pranced,
　Till it was nearly light!
And then their thoughts to supper
　chanced
To turn. (As well they might!)

Then said the Ant: "It's only right
　That supper should begin,
And if you will be so polite,
　Pray *take each other in.*"
(The emphasis was very slight,
　But rested on *"Take in."*)

They needed not a second call,
　They took the hint. Oh, yes,
The largest guest "took in" the
　small,
　The small "took in" the less,
The less "took in" the least of all.
　(It was a great success!)

As for the rest—but why spin out
　This narrative of woe?—
The Lion took them in about
　As fast as they could go.
(And went home looking very stout,
　And walking very slow.)

The Lion, bowing very low,
　Said to the Ant: "I ne'er
Since Noah's Ark remember so
　Delightful an affair."

[75]

(A pretty compliment, although
　He really wasn't there.)

And when the Ant, not long ago,
　Lost to all sense of shame,
Tried it again, I chance to know
　That not one answer came.
(Save from the Fish, who "could
　　not go,
But thanked her all the same.")

◇◇◇

SAMUEL HOFFENSTEIN

THE GNU

The gnu is a remarka-bul,
From all descriptions, ani-mul;
Yet how remarka-bul must you
Appear to the eccentric gnu!—
I have no doubt that even I
Must puzzle his peculiar eye;
There's something wrong with all
　of us;—
Let's ask the hippopotamus.

◇◇◇

OLIVER WENDELL
HOLMES

THE HEIGHT OF THE
RIDICULOUS

I wrote some lines once on a time
　In wondrous merry mood,
And thought, as usual, men would
　say
They were exceeding good.

They were so queer, so very queer,
　I laughed as I would die;
Albeit, in the general way,
　A sober man am I.

I called my servant, and he came;
　How kind it was of him
To mind a slender man like me,
　He of the mighty limb.

"These to the printer," I exclaimed,
　And, in my humorous way,
I added (as a trifling jest),
　"There'll be the devil to pay."

He took the paper, and I watched,
　And saw him peep within;
At the first line he read, his face
　Was all upon the grin.

He read the next; the grin grew
　broad,
And shot from ear to ear;
He read the third; a chuckling noise
　I now began to hear.

The fourth; he broke into a roar;
　The fifth; his waistband split;
The sixth; he burst five buttons off,
　And tumbled in a fit.

Ten days and nights, with sleepless
　eye,
　I watched that wretched man,
And since, I never dare to write
　As funny as I can.

From THE SEPTEMBER GALE

It chanced to be our washing day,
　And all our things were drying;
The storm came roaring through the
　lines,
　And set them all a-flying;
I saw the shirts and petticoats
　Go riding off like witches;
I lost, ah! bitterly I wept,—
　I lost my Sunday breeches!

I saw them straddling through the
　air,

[76]

Alas! too late to win them;
I saw them chase the clouds, as if
The devil had been in them;
They were my darlings and my pride,
My boyhood's only riches,—
"Farewell, farewell," I faintly
cried,—
"My breeches! O my breeches!"

That night I saw them in my dreams,
How changed from what I knew
them!
The dews had steeped their faded
threads,
The winds had whistled through
them!
I saw the wide and ghastly rents
Where demon claws had torn
them;
A hole was in their amplest part,
As if an imp had worn them.

I have had many happy years,
And tailors kind and clever,
But those young pantaloons have
gone
Forever and forever!
And not till fate has cut the last
Of all my earthly stitches,
This aching heart shall cease to
mourn
My loved! my long-lost breeches!

❖❖❖

THOMAS HOOD

From A PARENTAL ODE TO
MY SON, AGED THREE YEARS
AND FIVE MONTHS

Thou happy, happy elf!
(But stop,—first let me kiss away
that tear)—
Thou tiny image of myself!
(My love, he's poking peas into his
ear!)
Thou merry laughing sprite!
With spirits feather light,
Untouched by sorrow, and unsoiled
by sin—
(Good Heavens! the child is swal-
lowing a pin!)

Thou little tricksy Puck!
With antic toys so funnily bestuck,
Light as the singing bird that wings
the air—
(The door! the door! he'll tumble
down the stair!)
Thou darling of thy sire!
(Why, Jane, he'll set his pinafore
afire!)
Thou imp of mirth and joy!
In love's dear chain, so strong and
bright a link,
Thou idol of thy parents—(Drat the
boy!
There goes my ink!)

Thy father's pride and hope!
(He'll break the mirror with that
skipping-rope!)
With pure heart newly stamped
from Nature's mint—
(Where *did* he learn that squint?)
Thou young domestic dove!
(He'll have that jug off with another
shove!)
Dear nursling of the Ilymeneal
nest!
(Are those torn clothes his
best?)
Little epitome of man!
(He'll climb upon the table, that's
his plan!)
Touched with the beauteous tints of
dawning life
(He's got a knife!)

Thou pretty opening rose!
(Go to your mother, child, and wipe
  your nose!)
Balmy and breathing music like the
  South,
(He really brings my heart into my
  mouth!)
Fresh as the morn, and brilliant as
  its star,—
(I wish that window had an iron
  bar!)
Bold as the hawk, yet gentle as the
  dove,—
(I'll tell you what, my love,
I cannot write unless he's sent
  above!)

NO!

No sun—no moon!
No morn—no noon—
No dawn—no dusk—no proper time
  of day—
No sky—no earthly view—
No distance looking blue—
No road—no street—no "t'other side
  the way"—
No end to any Row—
No indications where the Cres-
  cents go—
No top to any steeple—
No recognitions of familiar people—
No courtesies for showing 'em—
No knowing 'em!
No traveling at all—no locomotion,
No inkling of the way—no notion—
"No go"—by land or ocean—
No mail—no post—
No news from any foreign
  coast—
No park—no ring—no afternoon
  gentility—
No company—no nobility—

No warmth, no cheerfulness, no
  healthful ease,
No comfortable feel in any
  member—
No shade, no shine, no butterflies,
  no bees,
No fruits, no flowers, no leaves, no
  birds,
November!

FAITHLESS NELLY GRAY

Ben Battle was a soldier bold,
  And used to war's alarms;
But a cannon ball took off his legs,
  So he laid down his arms.

Now as they bore him off the field,
  Said he, "Let others shoot;
For here I leave my second leg,
  And the Forty-second Foot."

The army surgeons made him limbs:
  Said he, "They're only pegs;
But there's as wooden members
  quite,
  As represent my legs."

Now Ben he loved a pretty maid,—
  Her name was Nelly Gray;
So he went to pay her his devours,
  When he'd devoured his pay.

But when he called on Nelly Gray,
  She made him quite a scoff;
And when she saw his wooden legs,
  Began to take them off.

"O Nelly Gray! O Nelly Gray!
  Is this your love so warm?
The love that loves a scarlet coat
  Should be more uniform."

Said she, "I loved a soldier once,
  For he was blithe and brave;
But I will never have a man
  With both legs in the grave.

[78]

"Before you had those timber toes
    Your love I did allow;
But then, you know, you stand upon
    Another footing now."

"O Nelly Gray! O Nelly Gray!
    For all your jeering speeches,
At duty's call I left my legs
    In Badajos's breaches."

"Why, then," said she, "you've lost
        the feet
    Of legs in war's alarms,
And now you cannot wear your
        shoes
    Upon your feats of arms!"

"O false and fickle Nelly Gray!
    I know why you refuse:
Though I've no feet, some other
        man
    Is standing in my shoes.

"I wish I ne'er had seen your face;
    But, now, a long farewell!
For you will be my death;—alas!
    You will not be my Nell!"

Now when he went from Nelly Gray
    His heart so heavy got,
And life was such a burden grown,
    It made him take a knot.

So round his melancholy neck
    A rope he did intwine,
And, for his second time in life,
    Enlisted in the Line.

One end he tied around a beam,
    And then removed his pegs;
And, as his legs were off,—of course
    He soon was off his legs.

And there he hung till he was dead
    As any nail in town;
For, though distress had cut him up,
    It could not cut him down.

A dozen men sat on his corpse,
    To find out why he died,—
And they buried Ben in four cross-
        roads,
    With a stake in his inside.

◇◇◇

A. E. HOUSMAN

THE SHADES OF NIGHT

The shades of night were falling fast,
    And the rain was falling faster,
When through an Alpine village
        passed
    An Alpine village pastor:
A youth who bore mid snow and ice
    A bird that wouldn't chirrup,
And a banner with the strange
        device—
    "Mrs. Winslow's soothing syrup"

"Beware the pass," the old man said,
    "My bold, my desperate fellah;
Dark lowers the tempest overhead,
    And you'll want your umberella;
And the roaring torrent is deep and
        wide—
    You may hear how loud it
        washes."
But still that clarion voice replied:
    "I've got my old goloshes."

"Oh, stay," the maiden said, "and
        rest
    (For the wind blows from the
        nor'ward)
Thy weary head upon my breast—
    And please don't think I'm for-
        ward."
A tear stood in his bright blue eye,
    And he gladly would have tarried;
But still he answered with a sigh:
    "Unhappily I'm married."

[79]

INHUMAN HENRY or CRUELTY TO FABULOUS ANIMALS

Oh would you know why Henry sleeps,
And why his mourning Mother weeps,
And why his weeping Mother mourns?
He was unkind to unicorns.

No unicorn, with Henry's leave,
Could dance upon the lawn at eve,
Or gore the gardener's boy in spring
Or do the very slightest thing.

No unicorn could safely roar,
And dash its nose against the door,
Nor sit in peace upon the mat
To eat the dog, or drink the cat.

Henry would never in the least
Encourage the heraldic beast:
If there were unicorns about
He went and let the lion out.

The lion, leaping from its chain
And glaring through its tangled mane,
Would stand on end and bark and bound
And bite what unicorns it found.

And when the lion bit a lot
Was Henry sorry? He was not.
What did his jumps betoken? Joy.
He was a bloody-minded boy.

The Unicorn is not a Goose,
And when they saw the lion loose
They grew increasingly aware
That they had better not be there.

And oh, the unicorn is fleet
And spurns the earth with all its feet.

The lion had to snap and snatch
At tips of tails it could not catch.

Returning home in temper bad,
It met the sanguinary lad,
And clasping Henry with its claws
It took his legs between its jaws.

"Down, lion, down!" said Henry, "cease!
My legs immediately release."
His formidable feline pet
Made no reply, but only ate.

The last words that were ever said
By Henry's disappearing head,
In accents of indignant scorn,
Were "I am not a unicorn."

And now you know why Henry sleeps,
And why his Mother mourns and weeps,
And why she also weeps and mourns;
So now be nice to unicorns.

WALLACE IRWIN

A DASH TO THE POLE

'Twas out on the Archipelago
In the region of the Horn,
Somewhere in the locks of the Equinox
And the tropic of Capricorn.

We bumped right into the Arctic,
Me and me matey, John.
We was near to frizz by the slush and the slizz,
For we hadn't our flannels on.

Who'd 'a' thought that a tried explorer
Would start for the Pole like that,

[80]

With openwork hose and summer
  clo'es
And a dinky old Panama hat?

We could see the Eskimoses,
  Far out on the ice ashore,
A-turnin' up of their noses
  At the comical clo'es we wore.

We could hear the bears on the
  glaciers
A-laughing kind of amused,
And there we stud in our seashore
  duds
A-looking that shamed and confused!

The whirl-i-gig Arctic breezes
  They biffled our bark abaft,
And the ice-pack shook with our
  sneezes,
  (For there was a terrible draft).

"Friend John," I yells to me matey,
  "Stand ready and warp the boat!"
But I suddenly found that John was
  drowned,
  And me alone and afloat.

I was chilled to the heart with terror
  At the loss of me matey, John,
I was chilled to the feet, for I beg
  to repeat,
  That I hadn't me flannels on.

When all of a dog-goned sudden
  A peak riz over the sun.
I swear on me soul 'twas the Arctic
  Pole—
  Then what d'ye think I done?

Then what d'ye think I done, sir,
  When that pinnacle swung in
  view?
I done what a wight in a similar
  plight
  With a similar Pole would do.

I swung the hand of the compass
  Till straight to the South points
  she,
And soon I divined that the Pole
  was behind
  And me in the open sea.

I landed next week at Coney
  Where I hitched me bark to a
  post,
Then I fell in a faint with pneumony
  Which I caught on the Arctic
  coast—

Out there on the Archipelago,
  In the region of the Horn,
Somewhere in the locks of the
  Equinox
  And the Tropic of Capricorn.

And that is why in summer,
  When it's most undeniably warm,
I dresses in felt and pelican belt,
  Which is suitable clo'es for storm.

And it's highly correct and proper
  To start for the Pole like that;
But I nevermore goes in me open-
  work hose
  And me dinky old Panama hat.

THE RHYME OF THE CHIVALROUS SHARK

Most chivalrous fish of the ocean,
  To ladies forbearing and mild,
Though his record be dark, is the
  man-eating shark
  Who will eat neither woman nor
  child.

He dines upon seamen and skippers,
  And tourists his hunger assuage,
And a fresh cabin boy will inspire
  him with joy
  If he's past the maturity age.

[81]

A doctor, a lawyer, a preacher,
  He'll gobble one any fine day,
But the ladies, God bless 'em, he'll
    only address 'em
  Politely and go on his way.

I can readily cite you an instance
  Where a lovely young lady of
    Breem,
Who was tender and sweet and de-
    licious to eat,
  Fell into the bay with a scream.

She struggled and flounced in the
    water
  And signaled in vain for her bark,
And she'd surely been drowned if
    she hadn't been found
  By a chivalrous man-eating shark.

He bowed in a manner most
    polished,
  Thus soothing her impulses wild;
"Don't be frightened," he said, "I've
    been properly bred
  And will eat neither woman nor
    child."

Then he proffered his fin and she
    took it—

Such a gallantry none can dis-
    pute—
While the passengers cheered as the
    vessel they neared
  And a broadside was fired in
    salute.

And they soon stood alongside the
    vessel,
  When a life-saving dingey was
    lowered
With the pick of the crew, and her
    relatives, too,
  And the mate and the skipper
    aboard.

So they took her aboard in a jiffy,
  And the shark stood attention the
    while,
Then he raised on his flipper and
    ate up the skipper
  And went on his way with a smile.

And this shows that the prince of
    the ocean,
  To ladies forbearing and mild,
Though his record be dark, is the
    man-eating shark
  Who will eat neither woman nor
    child.

SENSITIVE SYDNEY

'Twas all along the Binder Line
  A-sailin' of the sea
That I fell out with Sydney Bryne
  And Sid fell out with me.

He spoke o' me as "pie-faced squid"
  In a laughin' sort o' way,
And I, in turn, had spoke o' Sid
  As a "bow-legg'd bunch o' hay."

He'd mentioned my dishonest phiz
  And called me "blattin' calf"—

We both enjoyed this joke o' his
    And had a hearty laugh.

But when I up and says to him,
    "Yer necktie ain't on straight,"
"I didn't think ye'd say that, Jim,"
    He hissed with looks o' hate.

And then he lit a fresh segar
    And turned away and swore—
So I knowed I'd brung the joke too
    far
    And we wasn't friends no more.

THE FATE OF THE CABBAGE ROSE

They was twenty men on the Cab-
    bage Rose
    As she sailed from the Marma-
    duke Piers,
For I counted ten on me fingers and
    toes
    And ten on me wrists and ears.

As gallant skippers as ever skipped,
    Or sailors as ever sailed,
As valiant trippers as ever tripped,
    Or tailors as ever tailed.

What has become of the Cabbage
    Rose
    That steered for the oping sea,
And what has become of them and
    those
    That went for a trip on she?

Oh, a maiden she stood on the
    brown wharf's end
    A-watching the distant sail
And she says with a sigh to her
    elderly friend,
    "I'm trimming my hat with a
    veil."

A roundsman says to a little Jack
    tar,

"I orfentimes wonder if we—"
And the Jackey replied as he bit his
    cigar,
    "Aye, aye, me hearty," says he.

And a beggar was setting on Marma-
    duke Piers
    Collecting of nickles and dimes.
And a large stout party on Marma-
    duke Piers
    Was a-reading the Morning
    Times.

Little they thought of the Cabbage
    Rose
    And the whirl-i-cane gusts a-wait,
With the polly-wows to muzzle her
    bows
    And bear her down to her fate.

But the milliner's lad by the outer
    rim
    He says to hisself, "No hope!"
And the little brown dog as be-
    longed to him
    Sat chewing a yard o' rope.

And a pale old fisherman beat his
    breast
    As he gazed far out on the blue,
For the nor'east wind it was blow-
    ing west—
    Which it hadn't no right to do.

But what has become of the Cab-
    bage Rose
    And her capting, Ezra Flower?
Dumd if I cares and dumb if I
    knows—
    She's only been gone an hour.

◇◇◇

HENRY JOHNSTONE

THE FASTIDIOUS SERPENT

There was a snake that dwelt in
    Skye,

Over the misty sea, oh;
He lived upon nothing but goose-
berry pie
For breakfast, dinner and tea, oh.

Now gooseberry pie—as is very well
known,—
Over the misty sea, oh,
Is not to be found under every
stone,
Nor yet upon every tree, oh.

And being so ill to please with his
meat,
Over the misty sea, oh;
The snake had sometimes nothing
to eat,
And an angry snake was he, oh.

Then he'd flick his tongue and his
head he'd shake,
Over the misty sea, oh,
Crying, "Gooseberry pie! For good-
ness' sake,
Some gooseberry pie for me, oh."

And if gooseberry pie was not to be
had,
Over the misty sea, oh,
He'd twine and twist like an eel
gone mad,
Or a worm just stung by a bee, oh.
But though he might shout and
wriggle about,
Over the misty sea, oh,
The snake had often to go without
His breakfast, dinner and tea, oh.

JOHN KEATS

THERE WAS A NAUGHTY BOY

There was a naughty boy
And a naughty boy was he.

He ran away to Scotland,
The people for to see.
But he found
That the ground
Was as hard,
That a yard
Was as long,
That a song
Was as merry,
That a cherry
Was as red,
That lead
Was as weighty,
That fourscore
Was still eighty,
And a door was as wooden as in
England.
So he stood in his shoes and he
wondered,
He wondered, he wondered,
So he stood in his shoes and he
wondered.

BEN KING

THE PESSIMIST

Nothing to do but work,
Nothing to eat but food,
Nothing to wear but clothes
To keep one from going nude.

Nothing to breathe but air,
Quick as a flash 't is gone;
Nowhere to fall but off,
Nowhere to stand but on.

Nothing to comb but hair,
Nowhere to sleep but in bed,
Nothing to weep but tears,
Nothing to bury but dead.

Nothing to sing but songs,
Ah, well, alas! alack!

Nowhere to go but out,
Nowhere to come but back.

Nothing to see but sights,
Nothing to quench but thirst,
Nothing to have but what we've got;
Thus thro' life we are cursed.

Nothing to strike but a gait;
Everything moves that goes.
Nothing at all but common sense
Can ever withstand these woes.

IF I SHOULD DIE TONIGHT

If I should die tonight
And you should come to my cold
corpse and say,
Weeping and heartsick o'er my life-
less clay—
If I should die tonight,
And you should come in deepest
grief and woe—
And say: "Here's that ten dollars
that I owe,"
I might arise in my large white
cravat
And say, "What's that?"

If I should die tonight
And you should come to my cold
corpse and kneel,
Clasping my bier to show the grief
you feel,
I say, if I should die tonight
And you should come to me, and

there and then
Just even hint 'bout paying me that
ten,
I might arise the while,
But I'd drop dead again.

THAT CAT

The cat that comes to my window
sill
When the moon looks cold and the
night is still—
He comes in a frenzied state alone
With a tail that stands like a pine
tree cone,
And says: "I have finished my eve-
ning lark,
And I think I can hear a hound dog
bark.
My whiskers are froze 'nd stuck to
my chin.
I do wish you'd git up and let me in."
That cat gits in.

But if in the solitude of the night
He doesn't appear to be feeling right,
And rises and stretches and seeks the
floor,
And some remote corner he would
explore,
And doesn't feel satisfied just be-
cause
There's no good spot for to sharpen
his claws,
And meows and canters uneasy
about
Beyond the least shadow of any
doubt
That cat gits out.

THE COW SLIPS AWAY

The tall pines pine,
The pawpaws pause,
And the bumblebee bumbles all day;

The eavesdropper drops,
And the grasshopper hops,
While gently the cow slips away.

◇◇◇

EDWARD LEAR

THE NEW VESTMENTS

There lived an old man in the kingdom of Tess,
Who invented a purely original
dress;
And when it was perfectly made and
complete,
He opened the door and walked into
the street.

By way of a hat he'd a loaf of Brown
Bread,
In the middle of which he inserted
his head;
His Shirt was made up of no end of
dead Mice,
The warmth of whose skins was
quite fluffy and nice;
His Drawers were of Rabbit-skins,
so were his Shoes,
His Stockings were skins, but it is
not known whose;
His Waistcoat and Trowsers were
made of Pork Chops;
His Buttons were Jujubes and
Chocolate Drops.
His Coat was all Pancakes with Jam
for a border,
And a girdle of Biscuits to keep it
in order.
And he wore over all, as a screen
from bad weather,
A Cloak of green Cabbage leaves,
stitched all together.

He had walked a short way, when

he heard a great noise
Of all sorts of Beasticles, Birdlings
and Boys;
And from every long street and dark
lane in the town
Beast, Birdles and Boys in a tumult
rushed down.
Two Cows and a Calf ate his Cab-
bage leaf Cloak;
Four Apes seized his girdle which
vanished like smoke;
Three Kids ate up half of his Pan-
caky Coat,
And the tails were devoured by an
ancient He Goat.
An army of Dogs in a twinkling tore
up his
Pork Waistcoat and Trowsers to
give to their Puppies;
And while they were growling and
mumbling the Chops
Ten Boys prigged the Jujubes and
Chocolate Drops.
He tried to run back to his house,
but in vain,
For scores of fat Pigs came again
and again;
They rushed out of stables and
hovels and doors,
They tore off his Stockings, his
Shoes and his Drawers.
And now from the housetops with
screechings descend
Striped, spotted, white, black and
gray Cats without end;
They jumped on his shoulders and
knocked off his hat,
When Crows, Ducks and Hens
made a mincemeat of that.
They speedily flew at his sleeves in
a trice
And utterly tore up his Shirt of dead
Mice;

They swallowed the last of his Shirt
  with a squall,—
Whereon he ran home with no
  clothes on at all.

And he said to himself as he bolted
  the door,
"I will not wear a similar dress any
  more,
Any more, any more, any more,
  nevermore!"

INCIDENTS IN THE LIFE OF
MY UNCLE ARLY

O my agèd Uncle Arly!
Sitting on a heap of Barley
  Thro' the silent hours of night,—
Close beside a leafy thicket:—
On his nose there was a Cricket,—
In his hat a Railway-Ticket;—
  (But his shoes were far too tight).

Long ago, in youth, he squander'd
All his goods away, and wander'd
  To the Tiniskoop-hills afar.
There on golden sunsets blazing,
Every evening found him gazing,—
Singing,—"Orb! you're quite amaz-
  ing!
  "How I wonder what you are!"

Like the ancient Medes and Per-
  sians,
Always by his own exertions
  He subsisted on those hills;—
Whiles,—by teaching children spell-
  ing,
Or at times by merely yelling,—
Or at intervals by selling
  "Propter's Nicodemus Pills."

Later, in his morning rambles
He perceived the moving brambles
  Something square and white dis-
  close;—

'Twas a First-class Railway-Ticket;
But, on stooping down to pick it
Off the ground,—a pea-green Cricket
  Settled on my uncle's Nose.

Never—never more,—oh! never,
Did that Cricket leave him ever,—
  Dawn or evening, day or night;—
Clinging as a constant treasure,—
Chirping with a cheerious meas-
  ure,—
Wholly to my uncle's pleasure,—
  (Though his shoes were far too
  tight).

So for three-and-forty winters,
Till his shoes were worn to splinters,
  All those hills he wander'd o'er,—
Sometimes silent;—sometimes yell-
  ing;—
  Till he came to Borley-Melling,
Near his old ancestral dwelling;—
  (But his shoes were far too tight).

On a little heap of Barley
Died my agèd Uncle Arly,
  And they buried him one night;—
Close beside the leafy thicket;—
There,—his hat and Railway-
  Ticket;—
There,—his ever-faithful Cricket;—
  (But his shoes were far too tight).

THE TWO OLD BACHELORS

Two old Bachelors were living in
  one house;
One caught a Muffin, the other
  caught a Mouse.
Said he who caught the Muffin to
  him who caught the Mouse,
"This happens just in time, for we've
  nothing in the house,
Save a tiny slice of lemon and a
  teaspoonful of honey,

And what to do for dinner,—since
  we haven't any money?
And what can we expect if we
  haven't any dinner
But to lose our teeth and eyelashes
  and keep on growing thinner?"

Said he who caught the Mouse to
  him who caught the Muffin,
"We might cook this little Mouse if
  we only had some stuffin'!
If we had but Sage and Onions we
  could do extremely well,
But how to get that Stuffin' it is difficult to tell!"

And then those two old Bachelors
  ran quickly to the town
And asked for Sage and Onions as
  they wandered up and down;
They borrowed two large Onions,
  but no Sage was to be found
In the Shops or in the Market or in
  all the Gardens round.

But some one said, "A hill there is,
  a little to the north,
And to its purpledicular top a nar-
  row way leads forth;
And there among the rugged rocks
  abides an ancient Sage,—
An earnest Man, who reads all day
  a most perplexing page.
Climb up and seize him by the
  toes,—all studious as he sits,—
And pull him down, and chop him
  into endless little bits!
Then mix him with your Onion (cut
  up likewise into scraps),
And your Stuffin' will be ready, and
  very good—perhaps."

And then those two old Bachelors,
  without loss of time,
The nearly purpledicular crags at
once began to climb;
And at the top among the rocks, all
  seated in a nook,
They saw that Sage a-reading of a
  most enormous book.

"You earnest Sage!" aloud they
  cried, "your book you've read
  enough in!
We wish to chop you into bits and
  mix you into Stuffin'!"

But that old Sage looked calmly up,
  and with his awful book
At those two Bachelors' bald heads
  a certain aim he took;
And over crag and precipice they
  rolled promiscuous down,—
At once they rolled, and never
  stopped in lane or field or town;
And when they reached their house,
  they found (besides their want of
  Stuffin')
The Mouse had fled—and previously
  had eaten up the Muffin.

They left their home in silence by
  the once convivial door;
And from that hour those Bachelors
  were never heard of more.

From THE JUMBLIES

They went to sea in a Sieve, they did,
  In a Sieve they went to sea:
In spite of all their friends could say,
On a winter's morn, on a stormy day,
  In a Sieve they went to sea!
And when the Sieve turned round
  and round,
And everyone cried, "You'll all be
  drowned!"
They called aloud, "Our Sieve ain't
  big,
But we don't care a button! we don't
  care a fig!

In a Sieve we'll go to sea!"
   Far and few, far and few,
      Are the lands where the
      Jumblies live;
   Their heads are green, and their
      hands are blue,
      And they went to sea in a
      Sieve.

THE POBBLE WHO HAS NO TOES

The Pobble who has no toes
   Had once as many as we;
When they said, "Some day you may
   lose them all;"—
He replied,—"Fish fiddle de-dee!"
And his Aunt Jobiska made him
   drink,
Lavender water tinged with pink,
For she said, "The World in general
   knows
"There's nothing so good for a
   Pobble's toes!"

The Pobble who has no toes,
   Swam across the Bristol Channel;
But before he set out he wrapped
   his nose
   In a piece of scarlet flannel.
For his Aunt Jobiska said, "No harm
"Can come to his toes if his nose is
   warm;
"And it's perfectly known that a
   Pobble's toes
"Are safe,—provided he minds his
   nose."

The Pobble swam fast and well,
   And when boats or ships came
   near him
He tinkledy-binkledy-winkled a bell,
   So that all the world could hear
   him.

And all the Sailors and Admirals
   cried,
When they saw him nearing the
   further side,—
"He has gone to fish, for his Aunt
   Jobiska's
"Runcible Cat with crimson
   whiskers!"

But before he touched the shore,
   The shore of the Bristol Channel,
A sea-green Porpoise carried away
   His wrapper of scarlet flannel.
And when he came to observe his
   feet,
Formerly garnished with toes so
   neat,
His face at once became forlorn
On perceiving that all his toes were
   gone!

And nobody ever knew
   From that dark day to the present,
Whoso had taken the Pobble's toes,
   In a manner so far from pleasant.
Whether the shrimps or crawfish
   gray,
Or crafty Mermaids stole them
   away—
Nobody knew; and nobody knows
How the Pobble was robbed of his
   twice five toes!

The Pobble who has no toes
   Was placed in a friendly Bark,
And they rowed him back, and car-
   ried him up,
   To his Aunt Jobiska's Park.
And she made him a feast at his
   earnest wish
Of eggs and buttercups fried with
   fish;—
And she said,—"It's a fact the whole
   world knows,

"That Pobbles are happier without their toes."

THERE WAS AN OLD MAN WITH A BEARD

There was an Old Man with a beard,
Who said, "It is just as I feared!—
Two Owls and a Hen,
Four Larks and a Wren,
Have all built their nests in my beard!"

THERE WAS A YOUNG LADY WHOSE EYES

There was a Young Lady whose eyes
Were unique as to color and size;
When she opened them wide,
People all turned aside,
And started away in surprise.

THERE WAS AN OLD PERSON OF DUNDALK

There was an old person of Dundalk,
Who tried to teach fishes to walk;
When they tumbled down dead,
He grew weary and said,
"I had better go back to Dundalk!"

THERE WAS AN OLD MAN OF IBREEM

There was an old man of Ibreem,
Who suddenly threatened to scream:
But they said, "If you do,
We will thump you quite blue,
You disgusting old man of Ibreem."

HOW PLEASANT TO KNOW MR. LEAR

How pleasant to know Mr. Lear!
Who has written such volumes of stuff!
Some think him ill-tempered and queer,
But a few think him pleasant enough.

His mind is concrete and fastidious,
His nose is remarkably big;
His visage is more or less hideous,
His beard it resembles a wig.

He has ears, and two eyes, and ten fingers,
Leastways if you reckon two thumbs;
Long ago he was one of the singers,
But now he is one of the dumbs.

He sits in a beautiful parlor,
With hundreds of books on the wall;
He drinks a great deal of Marsala,
But never gets tipsy at all.

He has many friends, laymen and clerical,
Old Foss is the name of his cat;
His body is perfectly spherical,
He weareth a runcible hat.

When he walks in a waterproof white,
The children run after him so!
Calling out, "He's come out in his night-
gown, that crazy old Englishman, oh!"

He weeps by the side of the ocean,
He weeps on the top of the hill;
He purchases pancakes and lotion,
And chocolate shrimps from the mill.

He reads, but he cannot speak, Spanish,
He cannot abide ginger beer:

Ere the days of his pilgrimage
  vanish,
How pleasant to know Mr. Lear!

◇◇◇

HENRY S. LEIGH

THE TWINS

In form and feature, face and limb,
  I grew so like my brother,
That folks got taking me for him,
  And each for one another.
It puzzled all our kith and kin,
  It reached an awful pitch;
For one of us was born a twin,
  Yet not a soul knew which.

One day (to make the matter worse),
  Before our names were fixed,
As we were being washed by nurse
  We got completely mixed;
And thus, you see, by Fate's decree,
  (Or rather nurse's whim),
My brother John got christened *me*,
  And I got christened *him*.

This fatal likeness even dogg'd
  My footsteps when at school,
And I was always getting flogg'd,
  For John turned out a fool.
I put this question hopelessly
  To everyone I knew—
What *would* you do, if you were me,
  To prove that you were *you?*

Our close resemblance turned the
  tide
Of my domestic life;
For somehow my intended bride
  Became my brother's wife.
In short, year after year the same
  Absurd mistake went on;

And when I died—the neighbors
  came
And buried brother John!

HE! ME!

◇◇◇

NEWMAN LEVY

THE REVOLVING DOOR

This is the horrible tale of Paul
MacGregor James D. Cuthbert Hall,
Who left his home one winter's day
To go to work, and on his way
In manner that was strange and
  weird
Mysteriously disappeared.
He left no clue, he left no trace,
He seemed to vanish into space.
Now listen to the fate of Paul
MacGregor James D. Cuthbert Hall.

He worked, did James, as shipping
  clerk
For Parkinson, McBaine & Burke,
Who in their store on North Broad-
  way
Sold dry goods in a retail way.
And at the entrance to their store
There was a large revolving door
Through which passed all who went
  to work
For Parkinson, McBaine & Burke.

Upon this day, accursed of fate,
MacGregor James, arriving late
Dashed headlong madly toward the store,
And plunged in through the spinning door
Around about it twirled and whirled
And Paul was twisted, curled and hurled,
And mashed, and crashed, and dashed, and bashed,
As round and round it spun and flashed.
At times it nearly stopped, and then
It straightway started up again.
"I fear that I'll be late for work,
And Parkinson, McBaine & Burke
Will be distressed and grieved,"
      thought Paul
MacGregor James D. Cuthbert Hall.

He raised his voice in frantic cry,
And tried to hail the passers-by.
He tried in vain to call a cop,
But still the door refused to stop.
And so he spins and whirls about,
And struggles madly to get out,
While friends, heartbroken, search for Paul
MacGregor James D. Cuthbert Hall.

◇◇◇

JOSEPH C. LINCOLN

A COLLEGE TRAINING

Home from college came the stripling, calm and cool and debonair,
With a weird array of raiment and a wondrous wealth of hair,
With a lazy love of languor and a healthy hate of work
And a cigarette devotion that would shame the turbaned Turk.

And he called his father "Guv'nor,"
   with a cheek serene and rude,
While that raging, wrathful rustic
   called his son a "blasted dude,"
And in dark and direful language
   muttered threats of coming harm
To the "idle, shif'less critter" from
   his father's good right arm.

And the trouble reached a climax
   on the lawn behind the shed,—
"Now, I'm goin' ter lick yer, sonny,"
   so the sturdy parent said,
"And I'll knock the college nonsense from your noddle, mighty quick!"—
Then he lit upon that chappy like a wagonload of brick.
But the youth serenely murmured,
   as he gripped his angry dad,
"You're a clever rusher, Guv'nor,
   but you tackle very bad";
And he rushed him through the center and he tripped him for a fall,

And he scored a goal and touchdown
  with his papa as the ball.

Then a cigarette he lighted, as he
  slowly strolled away,
Saying, "That was jolly, Guv'nor,
  now we'll practice every day";
While his father from the puddle,
  where he wallowed in disgrace,
Smiled upon his offspring, proudly,
  from a bruised and battered face,
And with difficulty rising, quick he
  hobbled to the house.
"Henry's all right, Ma!" he shouted
  to his anxious waiting spouse,
"He jest licked me good and solid,
  and I tell yer, Mary Ann,
When a chap kin lick *your husband*
  he's a mighty able man!"

◇◇◇

FREDERICK LOCKER-LAMPSON

A TERRIBLE INFANT

I recollect a nurse call'd Ann,
  Who carried me about the grass,
And one fine day a fine young man
  Came up, and kiss'd the pretty
    lass.

She did not make the least objec-
    tion!
  Thinks I, "*Aha!*
  When I can talk I'll tell Mamma"
—And that's my earliest recollection.

◇◇◇

DON MARQUIS

A SEASIDE ROMANCE

"My name," I said, "is Peleg Dod-
    dleding,
  And Doddleding has been my
    name since birth."
And having told the girl this shame-
    ful thing
  I bowed my head and waited for
    her mirth.

She did not laugh. I looked at her,
    and she,
  With wistful gladness in her yel-
    low eyes,
Swept with her gradual gaze the
    mocking sea.
  Then dried her gaze and swept
    the scornful skies.

I thought perhaps she had not heard
    aright.
  "My name," I said, "is Doddle-
    ding!"
Thinking she would reply, "Ah,
    then, goodnight—
  No love of mine round such a
    name could cling!"

We'd met upon the beach an hour
    before,
  And our loves leapt together,
    flame and flame.
I loved. She loved. We loved. "She'll
    love no more,"

I moaned, "when she learns Doddleding's my name!"

She was not beautiful, nor did she
seem
The sort of person likely to be
good;
Her outcast manner 'twas that bade
me dream
If *anyone* could stand my name
she could.

She seemed a weakly sentimental
thing,
Vicious, no doubt and dull and
somewhat wried.
I said once more, "I'm Mister Doddleding!"
Feebly she smiled. I saw she had
no pride.

The westering sun above the ocean
shook
With ecstasy, the flushed sea
shook beneath. . . .
I trembled too. . . . She smiled! . . .
and one long look
Showed something queer had
happened to her teeth.

O world of gladness! World of gold
and flame!
"She loves me, then, in spite of
all!" I cried.
"Though Peleg Doddleding is still
my name,
Yet Peleg Doddleding has found
a bride!"

I stroked her hair. . . . I found it was
a wig. . . .
And as I slipped upon her hand
the ring
She said, "My name is Effie Mud-
dlesnig—

Oh, thank you! *Thank* you! Mister
Doddleding!"

In all the world she was the only one
For me, and I for her . . . lives
touch and pass,
And then, some day beneath a westering sun,
We find our own! One of her eyes
is glass.

THE JOKESMITH'S
VACATION

What did I do on my blooming
vacation?
I solemnly ate, and I frequently
slept;
But I chiefly live over in fond con-
templation
The days that I wept. For I wept
and I wept.

One making his living by humorous
sallies
Finds the right to be mournful a
blessed relief—
And hour after hour in the byways
and alleys

[94]

I sobbed out my soul in a passion
  of grief.

I'm really not humorous. (Cue to
    be scornful,
  Dear reader, and murmur, "We
    know that you ain't!")
And gee! what a treat to be human
    and mournful,
  As glum as a gumboil, as sad as a
    saint!

Anyone can weep tears when he
    suffers abrasion
  Of feelings or fingers or bunions
    or breeks,
But it hustles you some to find
    proper occasion
  When you have a year's weeping
    to do in two weeks!

Counting one evening my toes and
    my fingers
  I found them unchanged with the
    passing of years,
And I muttered, "How sad that the
    same number lingers!"
  And crept to my cot in a tempest
    of tears.

When I noted at morn that the sun
    was still rising
  To the eastward of things instead
    of the west
Its pathos so smote me 'tis scarcely
    surprising
  I tore at my tresses and beat on
    my breast.

I went to Niagara. Leaping and
    throbbing
  The waterfall fell, as per many
    an ad.
But over its roar rose the sound of
    my sobbing—

The water was moister, but I was
  more sad!

What did I do on my blooming
    vacation?
  Quite often I ate and I frequently
    slept,
But mostly I sobbed—I think with
    elation
  How I wept and I wept and I wept
    and I wept!

ARCHY A LOW BROW

boss i saw a picture
of myself in a paper
the other day
writing on a typewriter
with some of my feet
i wish it was as easy
as that what i have to do

is dive at each key
on the machine
and bump it with my head
and sometimes it telescopes
my occiput into my
vertebrae and i have a
permanent callous
on my forehead
i am in fact becoming
a low brow think of it
me with all my learning
to become a low brow

[95]

hoping that you
will remain the same
i am as ever your
faithful little bug

archy

From CERTAIN MAXIMS OF
ARCHY

i heard a
couple of fleas
talking the other
day says one come
to lunch with
me i can lead you
to a pedigreed
dog says the
other one
i do not care
what a dog s
pedigree may be
safety first
is my motto what
i want to know
is whether he
has got a
muzzle on
millionaires and
bums taste
about alike to me

THE HEN AND THE ORIOLE

well boss did it
ever strike you that a
hen regrets it just as
much when they wring her
neck as an oriole but
nobody has any
sympathy for a hen because
she is not beautiful
while everyone gets
sentimental over the
oriole and says how

shocking to kill the
lovely thing this thought
comes to my mind
because of the earnest
endeavor of a
gentleman to squash me
yesterday afternoon when i
was riding up in the
elevator if i had been a
butterfly he would have
said how did that
beautiful thing happen to
find its way into
these grimy city streets do
not harm the splendid
creature but let it
fly back to its rural
haunts again beauty always
gets the best of
it be beautiful boss
a thing of beauty is a
joy forever
be handsome boss and let
who will be clever is
the sad advice
of your ugly little friend

archy

THE HONEY BEE

the honey bee is sad and cross
and wicked as a weasel
and when she perches on you boss
she leaves a little measle

From ARCHY S AUTOBIOGRAPHY

if all the verse what i have wrote
were boiled together in a kettle
twould make a meal for every goat
from nome to popocatapetl
mexico

and all the prose what i have penned
if laid together end to end
would reach from russia to south
  bend
indiana

HUGHES MEARNS

THE LITTLE MAN WHO WASN'T THERE

As I was going up the stair
  I met a man who wasn't there!
He wasn't there again today!
  I wish, I *wish* he'd stay away!

THE PERFECT REACTIONARY

As I was sitting in my chair
I *knew* the bottom wasn't there,
Nor legs nor back, but I *just sat*,
Ignoring little things like that.

A. A. MILNE

BAD SIR BRIAN BOTANY

Sir Brian had a battleaxe with great
    big knobs on;
  He went among the villagers and
    blipped them on the head.
On Wednesday and Saturday, but
    mostly on the latterday,
  He called at all the cottages, and
    this is what he said:

   "I am Sir Brian!" (*ting-ling*)
   "I am Sir Brian!" (*rat-tat*)
   "I am Sir Brian, as bold as a
      lion—
      Take *that*—and *that*—and
      that!"

Sir Brian had a pair of boots with
    great big spurs on,
  A fighting pair of which he was
    particularly fond.
On Tuesday and on Friday, just to
    make the street look tidy,
  He'd collect the passing villagers
    and kick them in the pond.

   "I am Sir Brian!" (*sper-lash*)
   "I am Sir Brian!" (*sper-losh!*)
   "I am Sir Brian, as bold as a
      lion—
      Is anyone else for a wash?"

Sir Brian woke one morning, and he
    couldn't find his battleaxe;
  He walked into the village in his
    second pair of boots.
He had gone a hundred paces, when
    the street was full of faces,
  And the villagers were round him
    with ironical salutes.

[97]

"You are Sir Brian? Indeed!
     You are Sir Brian? Dear,
         dear!
     You are Sir Brian, as bold as
         a lion?
         Delighted to meet you
             here!"

Sir Brian went on a journey, and he
     found a lot of duckweed;
     They pulled him out and dried
     him, and they blipped him on
     the head.
And they took him by the breeches,
     and they hurled him into
     ditches,
     And they pushed him under water-
     falls, and this is what they said:

         "You are Sir Brian—don't
             laugh,
         You are Sir Brian—don't
             cry;
         You are Sir Brian, as bold as
             a lion—
             Sir Brian, the lion, good-
                 bye!"

Sir Brian struggled home again, and
     chopped up his battleaxe,
     Sir Brian took his fighting boots,
     and threw them in the fire.
He is quite a different person now
     he hasn't got his spurs on,
     And he goes about the village as
     B. Botany, Esquire.

         "I am Sir Brian? Oh, no!
         I am Sir Brian? Who's he?
         I haven't got any title, I'm
             Botany—
             Plain Mr. Botany (B)."

◇◇◇

COSMO MONKHOUSE

THE BARBER OF KEW

There once was a barber of Kew,
Who went very mad at the Zoo;
     He tried to enamel
     The face of the camel,
And gave the brown bear a shampoo.

THE GIRL OF NEW YORK

There once was a girl of New York
Whose body was lighter than cork;
     She had to be fed
     For six weeks upon lead
Before she went out for a walk.

◇◇◇

OGDEN NASH

THE LAMA

The one-l lama,
He's a priest,
The two-l llama,
He's a beast.
And I will bet
A silk pyjama
There isn't any
Three-l lllama.

ADVENTURES OF ISABEL

Isabel met an enormous bear;
Isabel, Isabel, didn't care.
The bear was hungry, the bear was
     ravenous,
The bear's big mouth was cruel and
     cavernous.
The bear said, Isabel, glad to meet
     you,
How do, Isabel, now I'll eat you!

Isabel, Isabel, didn't worry,
Isabel didn't scream or scurry.
She washed her hands and she
  straightened her hair up,
Then Isabel quietly ate the bear up.

Once on a night as black as pitch
Isabel met a wicked old witch.
The witch's face was cross and
  wrinkled,
The witch's gums with teeth were
  sprinkled.
Ho, ho, Isabel! the old witch
  crowed,
I'll turn you into an ugly toad!
Isabel, Isabel, didn't worry,
Isabel didn't scream or scurry.
She showed no rage and she showed
  no rancor,
But she turned the witch into milk
  and drank her.

Isabel met a hideous giant,
Isabel continued self-reliant.
The giant was hairy, the giant was
  horrid,
He had one eye in the middle of his
  forehead.
Good morning, Isabel, the giant said,
I'll grind your bones to make my
  bread.
Isabel, Isabel, didn't worry,
Isabel didn't scream or scurry.
She nibbled the zwieback that she
  always fed off,
And when it was gone, she cut the
  giant's head off.

Isabel met a troublesome doctor,
He punched and he poked till he
  really shocked her.
The doctor's talk was of coughs and
  chills
And the doctor's satchel bulged with
  pills.

The doctor said unto Isabel,
Swallow this, it will make you well.
Isabel, Isabel, didn't worry,
Isabel didn't scream or scurry.
She took those pills from the pill-
  concocter,
And Isabel calmly cured the doctor.

THE PURIST

I give you now Professor Twist,
A conscientious scientist.
Trustees exclaimed, "He never
  bungles!"
And sent him off to distant jungles.
Camped on a tropic riverside,
One day he missed his loving bride.
She had, the guide informed him
  later,
Been eaten by an alligator.
Professor Twist could not but smile.
"You mean," he said, "a crocodile."

THE OCTOPUS

Tell me, O Octopus, I begs,
Is those things arms, or is they legs?
I marvel at thee, Octopus;
If I were thou, I'd call me Us.

[99]

THE RHINOCEROS

The rhino is a homely beast,
For human eyes he's not a feast.
Farewell, farewell, you old
    rhinoceros,
I'll stare at something less pre-
    poceros.

ARTHUR

There was an old man of Calcutta,
Who coated his tonsils with butta,
Thus converting his snore
From a thunderous roar
To a soft, oleaginous mutta.

◇◇◇

JOSEPH S. NEWMAN

BABY KATE

Darling little Baby Kate
Poured her broth on father's pate.
Father hollered, "Hey, you goop!
That's my noodle in your soup!"

THE CONCERT

I left my chambers to attend
A concert by Iturbi
With nothing on but yellow spats,
A wrist watch and a derby.

Arriving early at the hall,
I entered with my house key
And chatted for a moment with
Debussy and Tchaikowsky.

I somersaulted past the guards
And hurried to the wicket . . .
A man obsequiously bowed
And handed me a ticket.

A diamond-studded usherette
Came swimming up to meet me;
I kissed her lightly on the cheek,
Requesting her to seat me.

The opening number filled me with
A most ecstatic feeling . . .
I floated lightly off my chair
And zoomed across the ceiling.

Encouraged by the loud applause
Of audience and musicians,
I tried a graceful loop-the-loop
Between the intermissions.

The news had spread across the
  town
And thousands were arriving . . .
I took off from the balcony
And did some power diving.

Iturbi grabbed me by the hand
And gave me an ovation . . .
I raised three tubas in the air
And flew them in formation.

A spotlight beamed me to the stage,
I landed down the middle
And finished my performance with
A handspring on a fiddle.

The crowds were milling through
  the aisles
And everyone was roaring . . .
I pulled the blankets to my neck
And presently was snoring.

❖❖❖

PRESTON NEWMAN

SOME QUESTIONS TO BE ASKED OF A RAJAH, PERHAPS BY THE ASSOCIATED PRESS

(AN EXCHANGE, FOR ONE VOICE
ONLY)

What's the greeting for a rajah rid-
  ing on an elephant?
  Howdah?
Howdah, Mistah Rajah, what's the
  weather like up there?
  Clowdah?
And, oh, Mistah Rajah, how does it
  feel to swing and sway
  without Sammy Kaye?
  What saye?
  Come lowdah?
And how does the rajah make an
  elephant staye

exactly where he wants him to?
  With an ankus?
Or do you tie a little rope around his
  anklus,
  so if anybody creeps up behind
    and shouts "Boo!"
  he still won't run awaye?
  You doo?
And lastly, Mistah Rajah,
  who takes care of the elephant
    when the rajah's not about?
  A mahout?
Thanku.
Rajah, over, and out.

❖❖❖

ALFRED NOYES

DADDY FELL INTO THE POND

Everyone grumbled. The sky was
  grey.
We had nothing to do and nothing
  to say.
We were nearing the end of a dismal
  day,
And there seemed to be nothing
  beyond,
        THEN
Daddy fell into the pond!

And everyone's face grew merry and
  bright,
And Timothy danced for sheer de-
  light.
"Give me the camera, quick, oh
  quick!
He's crawling out of the duckweed."
  Click!

Then the gardener suddenly slapped
  his knee,

[101]

And doubled up, shaking silently,
And the ducks all quacked as if they
    were daft
And it sounded as if the old drake
    laughed.

O, there wasn't a thing that didn't
    respond
                WHEN
Daddy fell into the pond!

⬖⬖⬖

WALTER PARKE

HIS MOTHER-IN-LAW

He stood on his head by the wild
    seashore,
And danced on his hands a jig;
In all his emotions, as never before,
A wildly hilarious grig.

And why? In that ship just crossing
    the bay
His mother-in-law had sailed
For a tropical country far away,
Where tigers and fever prevailed.

Oh, now he might hope for a peace-
    ful life
And even be happy yet,
Though owning no end of neuralgic
    wife,
And up to his collar in debt.

He had borne the old lady through
    thick and thin,
And she lectured him out of
    breath;
And now as he looked at the ship
    she was in
He howled for her violent death.

He watched as the good ship cut the
    sea,
And bumpishly up-and-downed,

And thought if already she qualmish
    might be,
He'd consider his happiness
    crowned.

He watched till beneath the hori-
    zon's edge
The ship was passing from view;
And he sprang to the top of a rocky
    ledge
And pranced like a kangaroo.

He watched till the vessel became a
    speck
That was lost in the wandering
    sea;
And then, at the risk of breaking his
    neck,
Turned somersaults home to tea.

THERE WAS A YOUNG PRINCE IN BOMBAY

There was a young prince in Bom-
    bay,
Who always would have his own
    way;
    He pampered his horses
    On five or six courses,
Himself eating nothing but hay.

THERE WAS AN OLD STUPID WHO WROTE

There was an old stupid who wrote
The verses above that we quote;
    His want of all sense
    Was something immense,
Which made him a person of note.

⬖⬖⬖

M. PELHAM

THE COMICAL GIRL

There was a child, as I have been
    told,

[102]

Who when she was young didn't
    look very old.
Another thing, too, some people
    have said,
At the top of her body there grew
    out a head;
And what perhaps might make some
    people stare
Her little bald pate was all covered
    with hair.
Another strange thing which made
    gossipers talk,
Was that she often attempted to
    walk.
And then, do you know, she occa-
    sioned much fun
By moving so fast as sometimes to
    run.
Nay, indeed, I have heard that some
    people say
She often would smile and often
    would play.
And what is a fact, though it seems
    very odd,
She had monstrous dislike to the
    feel of a rod.
This strange little child sometimes
    hungry would be
And then she delighted her victuals
    to see.
Even drink she would swallow, and
    though strange it appears
Whenever she listened it was with
    her ears.
With her eyes she could see, and
    strange to relate
Her peepers were placed in front of
    her pate.
There, too, was her mouth and also
    her nose,
And on her two feet were placed her
    ten toes

Her teeth, I've been told, were fixed
    in her gums,
And beside having fingers she also
    had thumbs.
A droll child she therefore most
    surely must be,
For not being blind she was able to
    see.
One circumstance more had slipped
    from my mind
Which is when not cross she always
    was kind.
And, strangest of any that yet I have
    said,
She every night went to sleep on her
    bed.
And, what may occasion you no
    small surprise,
When napping, she always shut
    close up her eyes.

◇◇◇

WILLIAM PITT

THE SAILOR'S
CONSOLATION

One night came on a hurricane,
    The sea was mountains rolling,
When Barney Buntline turned his
    quid,
    And said to Billy Bowling:
"A strong nor'wester's blowing, Bill;
    Hark! don't ye hear it roar now?
Lord help 'em, how I pities them
    Unhappy folks on shore now!

"Foolhardy chaps who live in towns,
    What danger they are all in,
And now lie quaking in their beds,
    For fear the roof shall fall in:
Poor creatures! how they envies us,
    And wishes, I've a notion,

For our good luck, in such a storm,
To be upon the ocean!

"And as for them who're out all day
On business from their houses,
And late at night are coming home,
To cheer their babes and
spouses,—
While you and I, Bill, on the deck
Are comfortably lying,
My eyes! what tiles and chimney-
pots
About their heads are flying!

"And very often have we heard
How men are killed and undone
By overturns of carriages,
By thieves and fires in London.
We know what risks all landsmen
run,
From nobleman to tailors;
Then, Bill, let us thank Providence
That you and I are sailors."

❖❖❖

ANNA M. PRATT

A MORTIFYING MISTAKE

I studied my tables over and over,
and backward and forward, too;
But I couldn't remember six times
nine, and I didn't know what to
do,
Till sister told me to play with my
doll, and not to bother my head,
"If you call her 'Fifty-four' for a
while, you'll learn it by heart,"
she said.

So I took my favorite, Mary Ann
(though I thought 'twas a dreadful shame
To give such a perfectly lovely child
such a perfectly horrid name),

And I called her my dear little
"Fifty-four" a hundred times, till
I knew
The answer of six times nine as well
as the answer of two times two.

Next day Elizabeth Wigglesworth,
who always acts so proud,
Said, "Six times nine is Fifty-two,"
and I nearly laughed aloud!
But I wished I hadn't when teacher
said, "Now Dorothy, tell if you
can."
For I thought of my doll and—sakes
alive!—I answered, "*Mary Ann!*"

❖❖❖

TOM PRIDEAUX

SKIP-SCOOP-ANELLIE

On the island of Skip-scoop-anellie
There is made every known kind of
jelly;
Kumquat and pineapple, citron and
quince,
Pomegranate, apricot, all are made
since
Someone discovered that jellyfish
ate
Fruit from a fishhook as though it
were bait.
Any particular jelly you wish,
Lower the fruit to the jellyfied fish,
After you've given it time to digest
Pull up the jellyfish. You know the
rest.

❖❖❖

A. T. QUILLER-COUCH

SAGE COUNSEL

The lion is the beast to fight,
He leaps along the plain,

[104]

And if you run with all your might,
He runs with all his mane.
I'm glad I'm not a Hottentot,
But if I were, with outward
cal-lum
I'd either faint upon the spot
Or hie me up a leafy pal-lum.

The chamois is the beast to hunt;
He's fleeter than the wind,
And when the chamois is in front,
The hunter is behind.
The Tyrolese make famous
cheese
And hunt the chamois o'er the
chaz-zums;
I'd choose the former if you
please,
For precipices give me spaz-
zums.

The polar bear will make a rug
Almost as white as snow;
But if he gets you in his hug,
He rarely lets you go.
And polar ice looks very nice
With all the colors of a pris-
sum;
But, if you'll follow my advice,

Stay home and learn your
catechis-sum.

◇◇◇

SIR WALTER RALEIGH

THE WISHES OF AN ELDERLY MAN

Wished At A Garden Party, June 1914

I wish I loved the Human Race;
I wish I loved its silly face;
I wish I liked the way it walks;
I wish I liked the way it talks;
And when I'm introduced to one
I wish I thought *What Jolly Fun!*

◇◇◇

WILLIAM BRIGHTLY RANDS

From CLEAN CLARA

What! not know our Clean Clara?
Why, the hot folks in Sahara,
And the cold Esquimaux,
Our little Clara knows!
Clean Clara, the Poet sings,
Cleaned a hundred thousand things!

She cleaned the keys of the harpsi-
chord,
She cleaned the hilt of the family
sword,

[105]

She cleaned my lady, she cleaned
   my lord,
All the pictures in their frames,
Knights with daggers and stomach-
   ered dames—
Cecils, Godfreys, Montforts,
   Graemes,
Winifreds—all those nice old names!
She cleaned the works of the eight-
   day clock,
She cleaned the spring of a secret
   lock,
She cleaned the mirror, she cleaned
   the cupboard,
All the books she India-rubbered!
She cleaned the Dutch tiles in the
   place,
She cleaned some very old-fashioned
   lace;
The Countess of Miniver came to
   her,
"Pray, my dear, will you clean my
   fur?"
All her cleanings are admirable,
To count your teeth you will be able,
If you look in the walnut table.

She cleaned the cage of the cocka-
   too,
The oldest bird that ever grew;
I should say a thousand years old
   would do.
I'm sure he looked it, but nobody
   knew;
She cleaned the china, she cleaned
   the delf,
She cleaned the baby, she cleaned
   herself!

Tomorrow morning, she means to
   try
To clean the cobwebs from the sky;
Some people say the girl will rue it,
But my belief is she will do it.

So I've made up my mind to be
   there to see
There's a beautiful place in the walnut tree;
The bough is as firm as a solid rock;
She brings out her broom at six
   o'clock.

◇◇◇

LAURA E. RICHARDS

IN FOREIGN PARTS

When I lived in Singapore,
It was something of a bore
To receive the bulky Begums who
   came trundling to my door;
They kept getting into tangles
With their bingle-bongle-bangles,
And the tiger used to bite them as
   he sat upon the floor.

When I lived in Timbuctoo,
Almost every one I knew
Used to play upon the sackbut, sing-
   ing "toodle-doodle-doo,"
And they made ecstatic ballads,
And consumed seductive salads,
Made of chickory and hickory and
   other things that grew.

When I lived in Rotterdam,
I possessed a spotted ram,
Who would never feed on anything
   but hollyhocks and ham;
But one day he butted down
All the magnates of the town,
So they slew him, though I knew
   him to be gentle as a lamb.
          But!
When I got to Kandahar,
It was very, very far,
And the people came and said to me,
   "How *very* plain you are!"

So I sailed across the foam,
And I toddle-waddled home,
And no more I'll go a-rovering be-
    yond the harbor bar.

THE SHARK

Oh! blithe and merrily sang the
    shark,
  As he sat on the house-top high:
A-cleaning his boots, and smoking
    cheroots,
  With a single glass in his eye.

With Martin and Day he polished
    away,
  And a smile on his face did glow,
As merry and bold the chorus he
    trolled
  Of "Gobble-em-upsky ho!"

He sang so loud, he astonished the
    crowd
  Which gathered from far and
    near.
For they said, "Such a sound, in the
    country round,
  We never, no, never did hear."

He sang of the ships that he'd eaten
    like chips
  In the palmy days of his youth.
And he added, "If you don't believe
    it is true,
  Pray examine my wisdom tooth!"

He sang of the whales who'd have
    given their tails
  For a glance of his raven eye.
And the swordfish, too, who their
    weapons all drew,
  And swor'd for his sake they'd die.

And he sang about wrecks and hur-
    ricane decks
  And the mariner's perils and
    pains,

Till every man's blood up on end
    it stood,
  And their hair ran cold in their
    veins.

But blithe as a lark the merry old
    shark,
  He sat on the sloping roof.
Though he said, "It is queer that no
    one draws near
  To examine my wisdom toof!"

And he carolled away, by night and
    by day,
  Until he made every one ill.
And I'll wager a crown that unless
    he's come down,
  He is probably carolling still.

MRS. SNIPKIN AND
MRS. WOBBLECHIN

Skinny Mrs. Snipkin,
  With her little pipkin,
Sat by the fireside a-warming of her
    toes.
  Fat Mrs. Wobblechin,
  With her little doublechin,
Sat by the window a-cooling of her
    nose.

Says this one to that one,
  "Oh! you silly fat one,
Will you shut the window down?
    You're freezing me to death!"
Says that one to t'other one,
  "Good gracious, how you bother
    one!
There isn't air enough for me to
    draw my precious breath!"

Skinny Mrs. Snipkin,
  Took her little pipkin,
Threw it straight across the room
    as hard as she could throw;
  Hit Mrs. Wobblechin

[107]

On her little doublechin,
And out of the window a-tumble
    she did go.

ANTONIO

Antonio, Antonio,
Was tired of living alonio.
    He thought he would woo
    Miss Lissamy Lou,
Miss Lissamy Lucy Molonio.

Antonio, Antonio,
Rode off on his polo-ponio.
    He found the fair maid
    In a bowery shade,
A-sitting and knitting alonio.

Antonio, Antonio,
Said, "If you will be my ownio,
    I'll love you true,
    And I'll buy for you,
An icery creamery conio!"

"Oh, nonio, Antonio!
You're far too bleak and bonio!
    And all that I wish,
    You singular fish,
Is that you will quickly begonio."

Antonio, Antonio,
He uttered a dismal moanio;
    Then ran off and hid
    (Or I'm told that he did)
In the Antarctical Zonio.

◇◇◇

E. V. RIEU

HALL AND KNIGHT or
$$z + b + x = y + b + z$$

When he was young his cousins used
    to say of Mr. Knight:
"This boy will write an Algebra—or

looks as if he might."
And sure enough, when Mr. Knight
    had grown to be a man,
He purchased pen and paper and an
    inkpot, and began.

But he very soon discovered that he
    couldn't write at all,
And his heart was filled with yearn-
    ings for a certain Mr. Hall;
Till, after many years of doubt, he
    sent his friend a card:
"Have tried to write an Algebra, but
    find it very hard."

Now Mr. Hall himself had tried to
    write a book for schools,
But suffered from a handicap: he
    didn't know the rules.
So when he heard from Mr. Knight
    and understood his gist,
He answered him by telegram: "De-
    lighted to assist."

So Mr. Hall and Mr. Knight they
    took a house together,
And they worked away at algebra in
    any kind of weather,
Determined not to give it up until
    they had evolved
A problem so constructed that it
    never could be solved.

"How hard it is," said Mr. Knight,
    "to hide the fact from youth
That x and y are equal: it is such an
    obvious truth!"
"It is," said Mr. Hall, "but if we
    gave a b to each,
We'd put the problem well beyond
    our little victims' reach.

"Or are you anxious, Mr. Knight,
    lest any boy should see
The utter superfluity of this repeated
    b?"

"I scarcely fear it," he replied, and
    scratched his grizzled head,
"But perhaps it *would* be safer if to
    b we added *z*."

"A brilliant stroke!" said Hall, and
    added *z* to either side;
Then looked at his accomplice with
    a flush of happy pride.
And Knight, he winked at Hall (a
    very pardonable lapse),
And they printed off the Algebra
    and sold it to the chaps.

◇◇◇

JAMES WHITCOMB RILEY

THE MAN IN THE MOON

Said the Raggedy Man on a hot
    afternoon,
  "My!
    Sakes!
      What a lot o' mistakes
Some little folks makes on the Man
    in the Moon!
But people that's been up to see him
    like Me,
And calls on him frequent and in-
    timutly,
Might drop a few hints that would
    interest you
  Clean!
    Through!
      If you wanted 'em to—
Some actual facts that might inter-
    est you!

"O the Man in the Moon has a crick
    in his back;
  Whee!
    Whimm!
      Ain't you sorry for him?
And a mole on his nose that is pur-

ple and black;
And his eyes are so weak that they
    water and run,
If he dares to *dream* even he looks
    at the sun,—
So he jes' dreams of stars, as the
    doctors advise—
  My!
    Eyes!
      But isn't he wise—
To jes' dream of stars, as the doctors
    advise?

"And the Man in the Moon has a
    boil on his ear—
  Whee!
    Whing!
      What a singular thing!
I know! but these facts are authentic,
    my dear,—
There's a boil on his ear; and a corn
    on his chin,—
He calls it a dimple,—but dimples
    stick in,—
Yet it might be a dimple turned
    over, you know!
  Whang!
    Ho!
      Why certainly so!—
It might be a dimple turned over,
    you know!

"And the Man in the Moon has a
    rheumatic knee,
  Gee!
    Whizz!
      What a pity that is!
And his toes have worked round
    where his heels ought to be.
So whenever he wants to go North
    he goes South,
And comes back with the porridge
    crumbs all round his
    mouth,

And he brushes them off with a
Japanese fan,
Whing!
Whann!
What a marvellous man!
What a very remarkably marvellous
man!

"And the Man in the Moon," sighed
the Raggedy Man,
"Gits!
So!
Sullonesome, you know!
Up there by himself since creation
began!—
That when I call on him and then
come away,
He grabs me and holds me and begs
me to stay,—
Till—well, if it wasn't for *Jimmy-
cum Jim,*
Dadd!
Limb!
I'd go pardners with him!
Jes' jump my bob here and be pard-
ners with him!"

◇◇◇

EMMA ROUNDS

JOHNNY

Johnny used to find content
In standing always rather bent,
Like an inverted letter J.
His angry relatives would say,
"Stand up! don't slouch! You've got
a spine,
Stand like a lamppost, not a vine!"
One day they heard an awful crack—
He'd stood up straight—it broke his
back!

◇◇◇

SIR OWEN SEAMAN

THE USES OF OCEAN

(Lines written in an irresponsible
holiday mood.)

To people who allege that we
Incline to overrate the Sea
I answer, "We do not;
Apart from being colored blue,
It has its uses not a few;
I cannot think what we should do
If ever 'the deep did rot.'"

Take ships, for instance. You will
note
That, lacking stuff on which to float,
They could not get about;
Dreadnought and liner, smack and
yawl,
And other types that you'll recall—
They simply could not sail at all
If Ocean once gave out.

And see the trouble which it saves
To islands; but for all those waves
That made us what we are—
But for their help so kindly lent,
Europe could march right through
to Kent
And never need to circumvent
A single British tar.

Take fish, again. I have in mind
No better field that they could find
For exercise and sport;
How would the whale, I want to
know,
The blubbery whale contrive to
blow?
Where would your playful kipper go
If the supply ran short?

[110]

And hence we rank the Ocean high;
But there are privy reasons why
    Its praise is on my lip:
I deem it, when my heart is set
On walking into something wet,
The nicest medium I have met
    In which to take a dip.

◇◇◇

JAMES A. SIDEY

THE IRISH
SCHOOLMASTER

"Come here, my boy; hould up your
    head,
    And look like a jintlemàn, Sir;
Jist tell me who King David was—
    Now tell me if you can, Sir."
"King David was a mighty man,
    And he was King of Spain, Sir;
His eldest daughter 'Jessie' was
    The 'Flower of Dunblane,' Sir."

"You're right, my boy; hould up
    your head,
    And look like a jintlemàn, Sir;
Sir Isaac Newton—who was he?
    Now tell me if you can, Sir."
"Sir Isaac Newton was the boy
    That climbed the apple tree, Sir;
He then fell down and broke his
    crown,
    And lost his gravity, Sir."

"You're right, my boy; hould up
    your head,
    And look like a jintlemàn, Sir;
Jist tell me who ould Marmion
    was—
    Now tell me if you can, Sir."
"Ould Marmion was a soldier bold,
    But he went all to pot, Sir;

He was hanged upon the gallows
    tree,
    For killing Sir Walter Scott, Sir."

"You're right, my boy; hould up
    your head,
    And look like a jintlemàn, Sir;
Jist tell me who Sir Rob Roy was;
    Now tell me if you can, Sir."
"Sir Rob Roy was a tailor to
    The King of the Cannibal Islands;
He spoiled a pair of breeches, and
    Was banished to the Highlands."

"You're right, my boy; hould up
    your head,
    And look like a jintlemàn, Sir;
Then, Bonaparte—say, who was he?
    Now tell me if you can, Sir."
"Ould Bonaparte was King of
    France
    Before the Revolution;
But he was kilt at Waterloo,
    Which ruined his constitution."

"You're right, my boy; hould up
    your head,
    And look like a jintlemàn, Sir;
Jist tell me who King Jonah was;
    Now tell me if you can, Sir."
"King Jonah was the strangest man
    That ever wore a crown, Sir;
For though the whale did swallow
    him,
    It couldn't keep him down, Sir."

"You're right, my boy; hould up
    your head,
    And look like a jintleman, Sir;
Jist tell me who that Moses was;
    Now tell me if you can, Sir."
"Shure Moses was the Christian
    name
    Of good King Pharaoh's daughter;

She was a milkmaid, and she took
  A *profit* from the water."

"You're right, my boy; hould up
  your head,
And look like a jintlemàn, Sir;
Jist tell me now where Dublin is;
  Now tell me if you can, Sir."
"Och, Dublin is a town in Cork,
  And built on the equator;
It's close to Mount Vesuvius,
  And watered by the 'craythur.' "

"You're right, my boy; hould up
  your head,
And look like a jintlemàn, Sir;
Jist tell me now where London is;
  Now tell me if you can, Sir."
"Och, London is a town in Spain;
  'Twas lost in the earthquake, Sir;
The cockneys murther English
  there,
  Whenever they do spake, Sir."

"You're right, my boy; hould up
  your head,
Ye're now a jintlemàn, Sir;
For in history and geography
  I've taught you all I can, Sir.
And if anyone should ask you now,
  Where you got all your knowl-
  edge,
Jist tell them 'twas from Paddy
  Blake,
  Of Bally Blarney College."

L. DE GIBERNE
SIEVEKING

THAT'LL BE ALL RIGHT
YOU'LL FIND

James has hated motorists ever since
  the day

They ran him down and broke his
  legs in such a heartless way;
OH, MY! There are some care-
  less men!
But what was worse than that
  was when
Poor Jimmy heard him say:
"That'll be all right you'll find!
That'll be all right you'll find!
No more trousers! No more
  boots!
Only coat and waistcoat suits
That'll be all right you'll find!
You'll walk upon your hands
  instead
And have more time to use
  your head,
That'll be all right you'll find!"

Mabel fainted right away, they
  thought that she was dead;
The dentist was shortsighted—
  pulled her nose clean off her
  head!
OH, MY! There are some care-
  less men,
But what was worse than that
  was when
He turned to her and said:
"That'll be all right you'll find!
That'll be all right you'll find!
It was a neat extraction, that,
And now you'd best put on your
  hat,
That'll be all right you'll find!
No more horrid colds and sniffs!
No more dirty handkerchiefs!
That'll be all right you'll find!"

  Rum-Tarrarra! Pom! Pom!

A SAD CASE OF MISAPPLIED
CONCENTRATION

The lion jumped over the desert;
(And I and my robin were there),

The palm trees turned pale when
    they saw it,
The mirage stopped working to
    stare,
The pyramid runkled with care.
But the men who were counting the
    sand
Quivered nor muscle nor hand
    For this incident rare
    Not a glance could they dare;
Never so much as an eyelid was
    winked, nor movement dis-
    placed a hair!

    For they were afraid
    They wouldn't be paid,
If a grain should be missed of the
    sum.
    And the camel perplexed
    As to what to do next
Made a noise with his nose like the
    sound of a drum
And spun round on his hump with
    his legs in the air;
    When the Lion jumped over
    the desert,
    (And I and my robin were
    there.)

❖❖❖

WILLIAM JAY SMITH

THE FLOOR AND THE
CEILING

Winter and summer, whatever the
    weather,
The Floor and the Ceiling were
    happy together
In a quaint little house on the out-
    skirts of town
With the Floor looking up and the
    Ceiling looking down.

The Floor bought the Ceiling an
    ostrich-plumed hat,
And they dined upon drippings of
    bacon fat,
Diced artichoke-hearts and cottage
    cheese
And hundreds of other such delica-
    cies.

On a screened-in porch in early
    spring
They would sit at the player piano
    and sing.
When the Floor cried in French,
    "Ah, *je vous adore!*"
The Ceiling replied, "You adorable
    Floor!"

The years went by as the years they
    will,
And each little thing was fine until ·
One evening enjoying their bacon
    fat,
The Floor and the Ceiling had a
    terrible spat.

The Ceiling, loftily looking down,
Said, "You are the *lowest* Floor in
    this town!"
The Floor, looking up with a fright-
    ening grin,
Said, "Keep up your chatter, and
    you will cave in!"

So they went off to bed: while the
    Floor settled down,
The Ceiling packed up her gay wall-
    flower gown;
And tiptoeing out past the Chip-
    pendale chair
And the gate-leg table, down the
    stair,

Took a coat from the hook and a
    hat from the rack,

And flew out the door—farewell to
the Floor!—
And flew out the door, and was seen
no more,
And flew out the door, and *never*
came back!

In a quaint little house on the out-
skirts of town,
Now the shutters go bang, and the
walls tumble down;
And the roses in summer run wild
through the room,
But blooming for no one, then why
should they bloom?

For what is a Floor now that bram-
bles have grown
Over window and woodwork and
chimney of stone?
For what is a Floor when the Floor
stands alone?
And what is a Ceiling when the
Ceiling has flown?

THE TOASTER

A silver-scaled dragon with jaws
flaming red

Sits at my elbow and toasts my
bread.
I hand him fat slices, and then, one
by one
He hands them back when he sees
they are done.

G. N. SPROD

REQUEST NUMBER

Tell me a story, Father, please do;
I've kissed Mama and I've said my
prayers,
And I bade good night to the soft
pussy-cat
And the little grey mouse that
lives under the stairs.

Tell me a story, Father, please do,
Of power-crazed vampires of
monstrous size,
Of hordes of malevolent man-eating
crabs
And pea-green zombies with X-ray
eyes.

GEORGE A. STRONG

THE MODERN HIAWATHA

He killed the noble Mudjokivis,
With the skin he made him mittens,
Made them with the fur side inside,
Made them with the skin side out-
side,
He, to get the warm side inside,
Put the inside skin side outside:
He, to get the cold side outside,
Put the warm side fur side inside:
That's why he put the fur side in-
side,
Why he put the skin side outside,
Why he turned them inside outside.

WILLIAM MAKEPEACE THACKERAY

A TRAGIC STORY

There lived a sage in days of yore,
And he a handsome pigtail wore;
But wondered much and sorrowed
more,
　Because it hung behind him.

He mused upon this curious case,
And swore he'd change the pigtail's
place,
And have it hanging at his face,
　Not dangling there behind him.

Says he, "The mystery I've found,—
I'll turn me round,"—he turned him
round;
　But still it hung behind him.
Then round and round, and out and
in,
All day the puzzled sage did spin;

In vain—it mattered not a pin,—
　The pigtail hung behind him.

And right and left, and round about,
And up and down, and in and out,
He turned; but still the pigtail stout
　Hung steadily behind him.

And though his efforts never slack,
And though he twist and twirl and
tack,
Alas! still faithful to his back,
　The pigtail hangs behind him.

DYLAN THOMAS

From UNDER MILK WOOD

Johnnie Crack and Flossie Snail
Kept their baby in a milking pail
Flossie Snail and Johnnie Crack
One would pull it out and one would
　put it back

O it's my turn now said Flossie Snail
To take the baby from the milking
pail
And it's my turn now said Johnnie
Crack

[115]

To smack it on the head and put it
   back

Johnnie Crack and Flossie Snail
Kept their baby in a milking pail
One would put it back and one
   would pull it out
And all it had to drink was ale and
   stout
For Johnnie Crack and Flossie Snail
Always used to say that stout and ale
Was *good* for a baby in a milking
   pail.

❖❖❖

NANCY BYRD TURNER

OLD QUIN QUEERIBUS

Old Quin Queeribus—
   He loved his garden so,
He wouldn't have a rake around,
   A shovel or a hoe.

For each potato's eyes he bought
   Fine spectacles of gold,

And mufflers for the corn, to keep
   Its ears from getting cold.

On every head of lettuce green—
   What do you think of that?
And every head of cabbage, too,
   He tied a garden hat.

Old Quin Queeribus—
   He loved his garden so,
He couldn't eat his growing things,
   He only let them grow!

❖❖❖

CAROLYN WELLS

HOW TO TELL THE WILD ANIMALS

If ever you should go by chance
   To jungles in the East;
And if there should to you advance
   A large and tawny beast,
If he roars at you as you're dyin'
You'll know it is the Asian Lion.

Or if some time when roaming
   round,
   A noble wild beast greets you,
With black stripes on a yellow
   ground,
   Just notice if he eats you.
This simple rule may help you learn
The Bengal Tiger to discern.

If strolling forth, a beast you view,
   Whose hide with spots is pep-
      pered,
As soon as he has lept on you,
   You'll know it is the Leopard.
'Twill do no good to roar with pain,
He'll only lep and lep again.

If when you're walking round your
   yard,

[116]

You meet a creature there,
Who hugs you very, very hard,
  Be sure it is the Bear.
If you have any doubt, I guess
He'll give you just one more caress.

Though to distinguish beasts of prey
  A novice might nonplus,

The Crocodiles you always may
  Tell from Hyenas thus:
Hyenas come with merry smiles;
But if they weep, they're Crocodiles.

The true Chameleon is small,
  A lizard sort of thing;
He hasn't any ears at all,
  And not a single wing.
If there is nothing in the tree,
'Tis the Chameleon you see.

A TUTOR WHO TOOTED
A FLUTE

A tutor who tooted a flute,
Tried to teach two young tooters to
    toot.
  Said the two to the tutor,

"Is it harder to toot, or
To tutor two tooters to toot?"

❖❖❖

HUMBERT WOLFE

THE ZOO

I scarcely think
    I like the Zoo
as much as other
    people do.

First when I see
    the elephants,
they seem in trouble
    with their pants,

and when the hippo-
    potamus .
says, "Who in blazes
    made me thus?"

And I observe the
    chimpanzee
thanking his God
    he's not like me.

While all varieties
    of cat,
make me feel dumpy,
    coarse and fat.

And that's not all!
    The eagles make
me stare as though
    my heart would break

at the great spaces
    of the air.
And why, it isn't
    my affair

if hippo is a
    sort of evil
joke perpetrated
    by the devil,

and of all broken-
    hearted things
the brokenest are
    captive wings!

And yet I can-
    not like the Zoo
as much as other
    people do.

◇◇◇

E. V. WRIGHT

WHEN FATHER CARVES THE DUCK

We all look on with anxious eyes
    When father carves the duck,
And mother almost always sighs
    When father carves the duck;
Then all of us prepare to rise,
And hold our bibs before our eyes,
And be prepared for some surprise,
    When father carves the duck.

He braces up and grabs a fork
    Whene'er he carves a duck,
And won't allow a soul to talk
    Until he's carved the duck,
The fork is jabbed into the sides,

Across the breast the knife he slides,
    While every careful person hides
    From flying chips of duck.

The platter's always sure to slip
    When father carves a duck,

And how it makes the dishes skip!
    Potatoes fly amuck!
The squash and cabbage leap in
    space,
We get some gravy in our face,
And father mutters Hindoo grace
    Whene'er he carves a duck.

We then have learned to walk
    around
    The dining room and pluck
From off the window sills and walls
    Our share of father's duck.
While father growls and blows and
    jaws
And swears the knife was full of
    flaws,
And mother laughs at him because
    He couldn't carve a duck.

◇◇◇

T. R. YBARRA

PROSE AND POESY: A RURAL MISADVENTURE

They roamed between
    Delicious dells,
He had sixteen
    Ecstatic spells.

He said: "Yon herds!
    Yon stretch of fence!
Yon frequent birds!
    Immense! Immense!

"Yon blossoms shy,
    Yon blazing sun,
Yon wondrous sky—
    Ai—! Ai—!

"My own, my sweet,
    Do you not glow
With bliss complete?"
    She answered "No!"

He stopped. He eyed
  Her in a trance.
He almost fried
  Her with his glance.

Then walked he East
  And walked she West,

His wrath increased
  As he progressed.

For who would wed
  With such a one
When all is said
  And all is done?

INDEX OF FIRST LINES

A boy who played tunes on a comb	29
A buttery, sugary, syrupy waffle—	21
A capital ship for an ocean trip	48
A centipede was happy quite	25
A decrepit old gasman, named Peter	29
A flea and a fly in a flue	29
A little girl with golden hair	30
A little peach in the orchard grew	57
A maiden caught stealing a dahlia	28
A raven sat upon a tree	53
A silly young fellow named Hyde	29
A silver-scaled dragon with jaws flaming red	114
A tutor who tooted a flute	117
Across the sands of Syria	68
After the day is over	34
An egg of humble sphere	24
An epicure, dining at Crewe	28
Antonio, Antonio	108
As a beauty I am not a star	57
As a friend to the children commend me the yak	31
As I was going up the stair	97
As I was laying on the green	24
As I was sitting in my chair	97
As I was standing in the street	23
Be kind and tender to the Frog	32
Ben Battle was a soldier bold	78
boss i saw a picture	95
Brian O'Linn was a gentleman born	26
Canst thou love me, lady?	38
"Come here, my boy; hould up your head	111
Crocodile once dropped a line	73
Darling little Baby Kate	100
De coon's got a long ringed bushy tail	26
Dog means dog	30
Everyone grumbled. The sky was grey	101
G stands for Gnu, whose weapons of Defence	31
Get up, get up, you lazy-head	22
He killed the noble Mudjokivis	115
He stood on his head by the wild seashore	102
He thought he saw an Elephant	40
He was, through boyhood's storm and shower	54
Here's to the man who invented stairs	73
Hezekiah Bettle was a bachelor of Maine	55
Home from college came the stripling, calm and cool and debonair	92
How pleasant to know Mr. Lear!	90
"How's your father?" came the whisper	26
I always eat peas with honey	23
I am	24
I give you now Professor Twist	99
I had written to Aunt Maud	23
i heard a	96
I left my chambers to attend	100

I met a traveller from an antique land 34
I never saw a Purple Cow 36
I recollect a nurse call'd Ann 93
I said, "This horse, sir, will you shoe?" 21
I scarcely think 117
I seen a dunce of a poet once, a-writin' a little book 36
I shoot the Hippopotamus 32
I sometimes think I'd rather crow 21
I studied my tables over and over, and backward and forward, too 104
I wish I loved the Human Race 105
I wish that my room had a floor 36
I wrote some lines once on a time 76
if all the verse what i have wrote 97
If ever you should go by chance 116
If I should die tonight 85
If Mary goes far out to sea 25
I'll tell thee everything I can 42
I'm a little Hindoo 25
I'm in a 1oder mood today 24
In enterprise of martial kind 63
In form and feature, face and limb 91
in Just- 55
In the family drinking well 28
Isabel met an enormous bear 98
It chanced to be our washing day 76
Itt rely is ridikkelus 58
James has hated motorists ever since the day 112
Jaybird a-sitting on a hickory limb 23

Johnnie Crack and Flossie Snail 115
Johnny used to find content 110
"Just the place for a Snark!" the Bellman cried 43
La-la-llamas rate as mammals 70
Lord Rumbo was immensely rich 27
Making toast by the fireside 67
Most chivalrous fish of the ocean 81
Most worthy of praise were the virtuous ways 52
Mr. Finney had a turnip 22
"My name," I said, "is Peleg Doddleding 93
My sense of sight is very keen 22
My son Augustus, in the street, one day 68
My typewriter, I gather 69
No matter what we are and who 70
No sun—no moon! 78
Nothing to do but work 84
O my agèd Uncle Arly! 87
Of all the ships upon the blue 62
Oh! blithe and merrily sang the shark 107
Oh, where the white quince blossom swings 74
Oh would you know why Henry sleeps 80
Old Farmer Buck, he bought him a duck 23
Old Quin Queeribus— 116
On the island of Skip-scoop-anellie 104
Once on a time an artful Ant 74
One night came on a hurricane 103
Poor old Jonathan Bing 35
Poor old lady, she swallowed a fly 22
Pop bottles pop-bottles 33

Said Mr. Smith, "I really can-
not 55
Said the Raggedy Man on a
hot afternoon 109
Sir Brian had a battleaxe with
great big knobs on 97
Skinny Mrs. Snipkin 107
So she went into the garden 57
Tell me a story, Father, please
do 114
Tell me, O Octopus, I begs 99
The *Ballyshannon* foundered
off the coast of Cariboo 64
The bravest names for fire and
flames 66
The cat that comes to my
window sill 85
The common cormorant or
shag 21
The conductor when he re-
ceives a fare 35
The gnu is a remarka-bul 76
The hippopotamus is strong 71
the honey bee is sad and cross 96
The lion is the beast to fight 104
The lion jumped over the
desert 112
The naming of cats is a diffi-
cult matter 56
The night was thick and hazy 49
The one-l lama 98
The ostrich is a silly bird 58
The Pobble who has no toes 89
"The proper way for a man
to pray" 58
The rhino is a homely beast 100
The rich man has his motor-
car 29
The shades of night were fall-
ing fast 79
The sun was shining on the
sea 40
The tall pines pine 85

The world has held great
Heroes 68
There lived a sage in days of
yore 115
There lived an old man in the
kingdom of Tess 86
There once was a barber of
Kew 98
There once was a girl of New
York 98
There wanst was two cats at
Kilkenny 25
There was a child, as I have
been told 102
There was a little pickle and
he hadn't any name— 48
There was a naughty boy 84
There was a snake that dwelt
in Skye 83
There was a Young Lady
whose eyes 90
There was a young man of
Herne Bay 28
There was a young man of
St. Bees 67
There was a young man so
benighted 28
There was a young prince in
Bombay 102
There was an ancient Grecian
boy 33
There was an old man from
Antigua 28
There was an old man of
Blackheath 29
There was an old man of
Calcutta 100
There was an old man of
Ibreem 90
There was an old man of
Tarentum 29
There was an Old Man with
a beard 90

There was an old person of
   Dundalk   90
There was an old person of
   Tring   29
There was an old stupid who
   wrote   102
There was once a giraffe who
   said, "What   74
"There's been an accident!"
   they said   67
They roamed between   118
They was twenty men on the
   Cabbage Rose   83
They went to sea in a Sieve,
   they did   88
This is the horrible tale of
   Paul   91
Thou happy, happy elf!   77
To begin with she wouldn't
   have fallen in   30
To people who allege that we 110
Tom Twist was a wonderful
   fellow   36
'Twas all along the Binder
   Line   82
'Twas on the shores that round
   our coast   59
'Twas out on the Archipelago 80
Two microbes sat on a pantry
   shelf   24
Two old Bachelors were living
   in one house   87
Upon a stairway built of brick 51
We all look on with anxious
   eyes   118
well boss did it   96

What did I do on my bloom-
   ing vacation?   94
What! not know our Clean
   Clara?   105
What's the greeting for a rajah
   riding on an elephant? 101
When a felon's not engaged
   in his employment   59
"When did the world begin
   and how?"   54
When George's Grand-
   mamma was told   32
When he was young his cou-
   sins used to say of Mr.
   Knight   108
When I lived in Singapore 106
When Lady Jane refused to be 72
When ski-ing in the Engadine 67
When the ploughman, as he
   goes   38
When they heard the Captain
   humming and beheld the
   dancing crew   49
When, with my little daughter
   Blanche   68
When you're lying awake with
   a dismal headache, and re-
   pose is tabooed by anxiety 61
Which I wish to remark   71
Willie poisoned Auntie's tea 28
Willie, with a thirst for gore 28
Winter and summer, whatever
   the weather   113
"You are old, Father Wil-
   liam," the young man said 39
Young Sammy Watkins
   jumped out of bed   28